LATER THOUGHTS
FROM THE SPRINGS
OF SILENCE

LATER THOUGHTS FROM THE SPRINGS OF SILENCE

BY

SISTER MARY GILBERT, SNJM

THE **BOBBS-MERRILL** COMPANY, INC.
A SUBSIDIARY OF HOWARD W. SAMS & CO., INC.
Publishers • INDIANAPOLIS • NEW YORK

NIHIL OBSTAT

John J. Coleman, *Censor Librorum*

IMPRIMATUR

Bernardus J. Topel, D.D., Ph.D.
Episcopus Spokanensis
May 5, 1962

For Thomas Merton
whose books gave me courage
to write this one
and for my mother

PREFACE

For an American in the twentieth century, few things are more difficult than the art of waiting. Citizen of an activist society, he demands and gets prompt service in every division of his public and private life, from three-minute car wash to instant coffee, from transcontinental jet flights to TV dinners.

This is the story of a long wait. To trap it between covers without taxing the reader's patience as much as the original experience tried ours, it was necessary to limit the time span. I have, accordingly, taken minor liberties with the sequence to include incidents that lay outside my chosen boundaries but were still part of the story. Similar selection with regard to characters has led me to reassign anecdote wherever it seemed consistent with personalities. This device has the advantage of providing an escape hatch for those whose privacy I have invaded.

The story is part travelogue—a journey into faith; part chronicle—the diary of a dream; part adventure—an encounter with reality. It blends the prose of everyday living with the poetry of God's ineffable designs. And always it is a human story in the fuller sense possible only to those who live in two worlds and who are aware of a supernatural dimension.

Because we are imperfect, we sometimes forget that "he who trusts in the Lord, makes the Lord his refuge . . . will be as well cared for as a tree planted by some river bank. . . . Still its green leaves defy the drought, and its fruit never fails." To learn the lesson, we must learn to wait. Our waiting will become the expression of our trust and the measure of our love. And when we have grasped that, the parts begin to fall into place like the pieces of a jigsaw puzzle, and we suddenly understand that "There is no riddle like the twists of the heart."

St. Mary's College
Notre Dame, Indiana
April 4, 1962

LATER THOUGHTS
FROM THE SPRINGS
OF SILENCE

CHAPTER I

Anyone who doubts that autumn is the perfect season has only to make his way across a college campus early in October. In the sharp morning air red leaves of the pin oak light up as if by miracle from the inside. To the reflective eye they symbolize the students before the ravages of winter strike, or the turbulence of spring. You can hear their animated laughter on a thousand campuses from Maine to California, where the echoes of young love catch at the ear and add their richness to the dying fall and flare. This is as good a place as any to take a closer look.

Color and movement crowd the walk that cuts diagonally across the sweep of lawn toward a low arcade joining two brick buildings. The arcade frames a vista of golden weeping willow, and the whole picture looks like something from the front cover of a college brochure. Youth and distances. This is the quiet season, edged with sadness because it cannot last, but transience is the quality that creates shadow and dimension in the whole.

When you move in a little nearer you can see the red plaids bright against squares of concrete walk and the sunlight making red glints in the dark hair of the girls. The legends on their faces read as gaily as the titles on

11

the paperbacks in their arms. Snatches of lighthearted talk carry over the clear air where the fragrance of perfume diffuses in the crisp scent of fallen leaves.

"This is the best time of all," you think, "millions of miles from the bomb that hangs over our skies and the sniping worries and compulsions that wear us down."

For what, after all, are the problems of late labs and early classes, of broken dates and closed weekends, of missed appointments and rejected papers? These are the golden years and every minute is precious.

The friendships formed here will probably outlast many others. The lessons learned here are larger than the memory. And the education begun here culminates only in eternity.

The students know this, too, but they seldom talk about it. Instead they look consistently forward according to the habit of the young. It is only you and I, from the vantage point of years, who dare to stop the moving camera and concentrate on stills. We are rewarded for our pains by being classified as sentimentalists, and perhaps we really are. If it is sentimental to be attracted by what is most alive and least mercenary we must plead guilty to the charge. For here, through this landscape of fall, walk the men and women America will become. We have bequeathed to them an education for survival, and it is the only weapon that knows no disarmament.

The success of their years here will depend in part on their motives and their maturity. We want the very best for them, and that is why we hope that they will take to college. It isn't something they do to mark time or stay

12

out of the service. It's their introduction (and only the introduction) to the life of the mind, the life that sets them apart from the vegetable and the merely animal.

Education is a weapon only in the sense that man himself is one. Or truth. Something that will protect him against that last and worst disaster, a life that has no meaning. But the centers in which this broad sort of education for survival is conducted are many and diverse. One of the strengths of American higher education has always been its lack of uniformity. Our colleges and universities are public and private, large and small, coeducational or not, expensively or moderately priced, exclusive or not on bases of social status, mental ability or scholastic achievement. Our leaders recognize that education is our first and greatest defense, that truth and freedom are our strongest weapons and must be assured to our young men and women.

What they do with the other weapons, if indeed they must do anything at all, depends completely on their years of service here. This is the real arsenal of democracy, and it is worth a long, long look.

The back-to-school scene is duplicated in millions of classrooms throughout the nation, though the circumstances and the personnel may vary. In nearly two thousand colleges and universities close to four million students have returned to classes, and more are on the way. What is it all about? And why is it so important? Is it something that could be accomplished without this elaborate system of formalities? And if it is, why do we bother? Or if it is not, what hidden power is at work here?

13

What goes on in higher education is as much concerned with what a man must *be* as with what he must *do*. That is why you do not go to college so much to become a hotel manager or a teacher or an account executive or a laboratory technician as to become a human being in the full sense. College leaves behind the primary preoccupation with tool subjects and with skills as such and moves ahead into that region where a man learns to relate and to judge, to weigh and evaluate, to be and to become. And it is in this broad inclusive sense that higher education is the prerogative of all intellectually competent human beings, regardless of sex, social status or economic position.

Higher education in a democracy is not something reserved for the wealthy. Still less does it belong only to descendants of the First Families. Nor can it any longer be the exclusive privilege of men.

Women now make up forty per cent of the total college population in the United States, and the proportion grows. In view of this fact, it seems superfluous to consider whether they belong in college at all. It's like holding a solemn discussion to decide whether we ought to have weather.

And since the number of marriages (as of divorces) continues to rise annually, there's not much point in talking about college education directed only toward a career. Whether or not American women follow a career for a time, the vast majority of them do marry, and if college is to be a woman's preparation for life, it must in some sense also be her preparation for marriage.

Look again at the familiar campus scene. Perhaps you

14

are the mother or father of one of these students. Perhaps one of them will be your future business partner. Or your partner for life. What difference will the years in college make? To understand, you will have to follow the crowd through the door to the building at your right. Classes have already been underway for twenty minutes.

In that large sunny room on the second floor forty college freshmen listen to a lecture on biology. This afternoon half of them will gather in the laboratory for their introduction to the materials and equipment they'll be expected to handle.

Down the hall a French professor gesticulates in the manner of Frenchmen everywhere while the class attends to words and motion to translate this intense personal enthusiasm for contemporary native writers.

Across the corridor a mathematician covers the blackboard with signs and numbers as calculus students strain to keep up with the rapidly moving chalk propelled by an even more rapidly moving brain and hand.

Next door a roomful of future teachers takes a quick look at the dimensions of elementary education in present-day America, and in the neighboring classroom alert eyes focus on a graph delineating the growth of selected social problems.

Education has a timeless quality. It gathers up the best from the past, applies it to the present, and thus creates and insures a future.

Down on the main floor the library looks like a bank on Saturday morning, and in the room beyond another thirty freshmen find out why they're here. Only *here*, in this case, refers not to the college but to the earth, for this is a class in theology.

For this is a Catholic college. The students are all women, and the professors, nuns.

CHAPTER II

Cab drivers in Spokane, Washington, (population, 181,000) always pretended they knew the way to Holy Names College. And sometimes they did.

More often they knew vaguely that it was out in that neighborhood dubbed "Piety Flat" where Bing Crosby had lived and gone to school and come back to dedicate Crosby Library, his gift to Gonzaga University. Behind the grey hulk of the administration building, the Roman letters over its entrance still reading "Gonzaga College, 1887," typewriters clicked and switchboard wires hummed. Farther down the block you came to Patrick Welch Hall, a slick modern building on a landscaped square, one of several steps in a Greater Gonzaga drive that had boosted enrollment to 1600 and spruced up the campus until old-timers scarcely recognized it.

The legend of Bing's academic career was almost as well known as the bald pate under the blond toupee, but everybody liked "Der Bingle" and townspeople turned out to see him accept an honorary degree, looking as much at home in a mortarboard as in the role of Hamlet. Afterward they pressed through the glass doors into the marble entry and up the library stairs to the Crosbyana Room to see the Oscars the crooner had won, review scenes from *The Road to Singapore* and *Going My Way*, and follow his song hits served up on fancy gold platters in locked showcases. His golf record was there, too, in trophy and picture, liberally sprinkled with Jesuit priests and local doctors and lawyers.

Cabbies still commented on the co-eds, a seventh-day wonder imported after World War II in the general panic over wartime enrollment drops. The women were there to stay, though, and after the first brave pioneers, the numbers grew every year. Book salesmen began to notice happy changes in business offices and personnel, and much of the nostalgic talk about football faded away.

Housing remained at a premium in a neighborhood where Catholic education for daughters was within walking distance from first grade through college. Though Gonzaga Prep had abandoned the ugly barracks in the shadow of the University, high school boys usually could manage their own transportation. So parents eyed their growing families and moved in to stay.

Five blocks east where Boone Avenue crossed Superior Street to come to a dead end next to the railroad track along the river, cab drivers hesitated. They might already have slowed past Marian Hall, a Holy Names College dormitory for one hundred women, but when they reached the intersection it was "Eeny meeny, miney, mo,/This is Institution Row."

To the left, across from Mission Park where neighborhood moppets gave the swings a sixteen-hour workout, loomed an architect's heirloom: four stories of towering brick supported by several iron fire escapes and encircled by a dense, discolored hedge. Across Boone to the right, a newer structure of simple lines, set far back from the sidewalk, presented an alternate choice. Beside it a tall gaunt building rose like a tomb where Superior Street pavement expired at the edge of a muddy path leading to some warehouses.

If the cabby were alert he noted small children playing in the back yard of the last building and narrowed his choice to two.

"That's the Academy to the left," the passenger might say.

The cab driver invariably pulled left.

"No, I'm going to the *College*. Just keep straight ahead to that yellow fence and then turn right. It'll take you to the arcade entrance."

The lesson would have to be repeated endlessly because so many who heard it really didn't care. Gonzaga men students were more interested but less diplomatic. They just took one look at the low two-story dorm hemmed in by family homes; at the long clean lines of the main building almost cater-corner, and asked:

"You mean this is the whole College? What's the enrollment?"

When they found out that it was one-fifth of Gonzaga's they felt even better than the day they discovered Whitworth's co-ed population was only three-fourths as large as their own. Sixteen hundred, twelve hundred, two hundred fifty. Small, smaller, smallest. And people so easily translated the terms into: Important, less important, unimportant.

If that was the way they looked at things they could

find more support for it in Eastern Washington College's 1,850 just eighteen miles away in Cheney; or in Washington State University's 5,900, not two hours distant in Pullman. Or in the University of Idaho's 3,700 across the state line from WSU.

But that was definitely not the way the faculties of the Spokane colleges viewed the matter. Presbyterian Whitworth, as an independent college committed to an ideal of Christian higher education, perhaps had more in common with the two Catholic institutions than with other types of colleges and universities. But faculty members from any one of the region's higher schools might have been among those applauding spectators at the Crosby Library dedication. For they were all interested in higher education, and they knew that in the United States its diversified pattern constitutes one of its principal strengths.

It would have been foolish to contend that just because our colleges were different from one another, they deserved to stay in operation. But each of us shared the conviction that our respective institutions could do something for a particular type of student, and that distinct educational roles justified our separate existences.

The quantitative measurement would have been hard on me personally as well. Five feet two in medium heels. Not much taller, the journalism students used to say, than a stick of dynamite. And I always answered that if they got a charge out of it, go right ahead, even though the comparison was imprecise for anyone so mild-tempered and reflective.

Actually, there wasn't too much time for reflection with

the assignments measured out for me: teaching classes in journalism and English, advising student publications, taking and processing pictures, writing college news stories.

I had heard of a smart metropolitan public relations man who prepared for a convention by talking his college into hosting a free breakfast for all the cab drivers of the city. With the royal treatment they had received there fresh in mind, the drivers taxied out-of-town delegates unerringly to their destination, dispensing information about the college en route. That was known as getting somebody else to do your work for you, and maybe I ought to try it.

I had learned the rationale for the women's college by rote over a period of years before and after my entry into the Sisters of the Holy Names of Jesus and Mary. Upon coming to Holy Names College to teach I had reviewed this rationale dutifully, recited it for visiting parents and students, explained it to uncomprehending colleagues and gradually come to believe it with an intensity of conviction based on a decade of critical examination and direct experience.

By this time the subject was so familiar to me that I could carry on both sides of the dialogue, anticipating the objections and wrapping them neatly into the presentation: "You may have thought that small colleges are exclusive, that women's colleges are geared toward homemaking, that Catholic colleges are devoted to religious studies. Well, they are and they aren't. . . ."

At Holy Names College we were often asked why we didn't withdraw in favor of Gonzaga. After all we were

21

both Catholic schools. Gonzaga was twenty years older than the normal school from which Holy Names College had evolved and senior by half a century to the liberal arts program we had introduced in 1939. The American trend toward big business evidently influenced the thinking of some critics who considered higher education a service too costly to maintain for two or three hundred women. They seemed to forget that we had automatically limited our prospects by more than half when we chose to exclude men. They probably hadn't heard of colleges like Scripps that held enrollment down to 250 women, though economic problems there had been solved in part by a cooperative system known as the Five Colleges Experiment.

But what they forgot was a basic difference in our philosophy of education. For we were one of 175 accredited colleges in this country based on the belief that the ideal education for women is one designed specifically for them.

Sometimes I tried to clarify my own thinking by preparing The Case for the Women's College in taxi talk.

"Some of the women's colleges started when there was no other place for women to go if they were interested in higher study. To begin with, the program of classes followed those in men's schools. But after a while educators began to experiment with different types of courses.

"Today nearly everybody agrees that college should keep pace with woman's widening role by preparing her for homemaking, for paid employment, and for community service. Educators disagree on the stress to be placed on each element. Champions of the liberal arts believe that the individual development they provide is the best preparation for all three roles."

By this time my audience on wheels was supposed to be steering straight for Holy Names College while he fed me the next cue.

"Don't they teach liberal arts at Gonzaga?"

Then I could tell him that of course they did. But even after women were admitted to most of the nation's colleges and universities, women's colleges continued to spring up and grow. They rested solidly on the conviction that higher education should recognize and cultivate:

1) The ways women differ from men psychologically, spiritually, physically.

2) The special role of women in society.

3) Women's tendency to learn and respond to teaching differently from men and differently in mixed classes from when they are alone.

If we hadn't come to a dead end inside the cab as well as outside I could then go on to explain the three distinctions, lapsing into pidgin or parrot out of sheer laziness, sprinkling my instruction with polysyllables to confuse and statistics to impress.

"Although psychologists still are interested in the problems of the woman's mind in relation to the various branches of learning, I am not really qualified to discuss that. I realize that it is quite possible that some of the apparent suitability of mind to subject matter may be culturally induced. One has only to read the Victorian novelists to discover that, at a time not too far distant,

Latin and Greek and languages generally were considered too taxing for the female constitution. Even the types of learning regarded as suitable were not to be pursued in depth. A woman might play some light tinkling numbers on the piano, but really serious music was out of the question. And in general her education included needlework, a smattering of French, polite literature and similar studies."

By now we would have reached the stoplight on Hamilton Street and I could point out the old three-story home, our Loretto Hall, that had been a supplementary dormitory off and on for nearly twenty years. When the green light was with me I knew I had about forty seconds left to finish my lesson.

"You'll have to come out to Holy Names College some time for a program," I'd suggest. "I'd like to show you around the College and have you meet some of our students."

I could see them coming toward us. Marian and Joan and Margaret and Cathy. They must be just getting out of biology laboratory because it was late afternoon and their cheeks were flushed. They were evidently comparing results of some experiment until one of them broke away from the group and began walking a little more eagerly. I looked back toward Marian Hall and saw a Gonzaga letterman on his extracurricular way.

The cab driver had seen him in the mirror, and I knew that I had found somebody else to do my work for me.

I could return to my reflections on the complementary nature of the sexes. Women are characteristically intuitive, interested in persons and in detail, disposed to the creative in all phases of human endeavor. Men, on the other hand, usually prefer the rational or logical. They are more interested in things. They are competent in handling activities that call for scope; they are better able to organize. It is largely on the truth or falsity of these premises that the case for educating men and women separately must rest, and I am aware that some educators today do, indeed, consider the entire foundation precarious.

Perhaps another century would see a dramatic upsurge in women mathematicians and scientists, as well as in lady lawyers and engineers. Perhaps the women's colleges would die—all 175 of them. Or go co-ed. That would be one hundred Catholic "funerals" or "weddings" since sixty per cent of the country's women's colleges are Catholic, most of them owned and operated by communities of religious women.

Baptists and Presbyterians conduct most of the twenty-one sectarian colleges for women. Thirty-seven are non-denominational; fourteen, state supported. I wondered how many persons in the thirty-five states and the District of Columbia knew anything about their women's colleges. The lines of communication might be more effective in New York with twenty-four, Pennsylvania with fifteen, and Massachusetts, eleven. California could match Ohio's nine and perhaps make some impact on the state. Down the line Virginia had eight; Wisconsin, seven; Texas, six; and there were five apiece in Georgia, Illinois, Michigan, Missouri and South Carolina. Till you came to the wide open West with only one women's college in each of the two remaining Pacific Coast states, Oregon and Washington.

Our Spokane College had had to build its reputation slowly and without major support from the local community. But when I looked at our students and our alumnae, I knew it was worth the effort. I would have been willing to match the best of them against the products of coeducation without concern over their academic or social competence.

Evidently Mr. Letterman shared my enthusiasm. Patterns of social behavior, I mused, tend to stress or minimize the differences between the sexes. And it's no secret that the average man is not particularly attracted by a masculine woman. Or the woman by a feminine man.

In our civilization today there is a predominance of the masculine or aggressive elements and a scarcity of the feminine and creative. Father Gerald Vann has discussed this condition at length in *The Water and the Fire*, and though he does not link it with the current trend to coeducation, I wonder whether there may not be a connection.

It would be ridiculous to suppose that a small Catholic college for women is the best choice for all, and surely the student's welfare ought to come first. I believe in being as objective as possible, given one's manifest loyalties, and letting the student make the decision for herself. Over and over experience has shown that to talk a student out of going elsewhere is a favor neither to her nor to the college. Education is a reciprocal process, and college and collegian may be critical of each other without malice or detriment. In fact constructive criticism can proceed only on a basis of mutual respect and sincerity.

Most colleges have students who transfer—in as well as out—and reactions on the part of both are mixed. Each of these cases strengthens the notion that college selection is a highly individual and important matter.

What kind of student goes to Holy Names College? All kinds. One of the most frequent observations made by faculty members after their first two or three months there is, "There's something special about our girls." Of course, as an educator, I hold that if a faculty didn't believe this to be true of the students it would be handicapped at the start. The act of teaching, if it is the personal relationship it should be, reveals to the teacher the good that is in every student, the image of the Creator in Whose likeness all are made.

Yet this conviction that its students are unusual seems stronger at Holy Names College than in many comparable institutions. Most of the students are, I think, attractively unsophisticated, friendly, earnest. But beyond that, there is a great deal of variety.

In a typical year, students come from nine different countries. The majority of the United States students are from the Pacific Northwest, though midwestern and eastern states are represented. Girls also come from Canada, India, Japan, Peru, Puerto Rico, China, Uganda, Thailand, and Tanganyika to attend Holy Names.

Academically, the students are not equal. Some of them rank in the top ten per cent of their graduating classes, but the college so far requires only a high school average of C for admission. In recent years entrance requirements have been stepped up in line with the nationwide trend, but the pupil-teacher ratio, the integration made possible through a unified philosophy, and the absence of certain co-ed college distractions during class hours at least, sometimes present fewer obstacles to scholastic success.

The majority of Holy Names College students are Catholic, though non-Catholics are free to attend and frequently do. Among the Catholics, vast differences of religious background exist, as many come from small, outlying communities where they have attended public high schools and have had little opportunity to live a full Catholic life. I can recall at least one student body president who was a non-Catholic, and it's consequently a little amusing when outsiders think of HNC as a female seminary.

I remember one time when I asked two of the students to help register delegates to a public relations convention for Northwest colleges and universities. One of the men was noticeably impressed with the spirited and gracious reception accorded him and asked the girl where she was from. When she mentioned Holy Names College, he noted with dismay that she wore an engagement ring and later took occasion to ask me how such a thing could be.

Once I had demolished the "seminary idea," we were free to launch into other topics, and he seemed amazed that anyone could really believe that an education geared to women might produce superior results. Evidently the sample convinced him, for he made detailed inquiries and promised to consider the replies when his own daughters reached college age.

There is, admittedly, a weakness in this logic. To ascertain what part of this student's charm was traceable to her college education, you'd have to find out what happened to her in another type of college—something we can only speculate about because she was one of those who chose and remained loyal to Holy Names while her brothers attended a co-ed university nearby.

Our best and most attractive students are those who come to us for positive reasons and remain even when there is a good deal of social pressure to lure them elsewhere. One of them was Ann, who worked on the Gonzaga switchboard through high school and college, turned aside all the teasing invitations to "go to a *good* school," and eventually married the Gonzaga man she'd been dating ever since she started to Holy Names. Her mother, also employed on the switchboard, probably knew everybody at the University, by voice if not by sight, and counted many friends among the faculty. She was one of the moving spirits in organizing our women's auxiliary, the Holy Names Colleagues, and continued to be one of its most energetic workers.

People used to ask us periodically when we were going co-ed, and the joke seemed less funny after one women's college in Oregon actually did it. But the truth is, nobody really wanted to get rid of the men completely. Women need the opportunity to contact men's minds, and we try to provide for that in the classroom and out of it. We hired several laymen as well as priests to teach classes. Intercollegiate organizations and social activities bring the students into mixed company. Evening classes are open to men, and dramatic productions tangle so inextricably with real life that I once wrote a newspaper story about Cupid on stage, detailing all the leading men who had been led to the altar as a consequence of taking bit parts or working on the stage crew.

Isolated from men, women students may become too passive, too willing to agree with everything instead of questioning what they hear. The alert instructor will be on the lookout for this intellectual deadness and will deliberately stir up some controversy if necessary. She will do whatever she can to stimulate the kind of independent thought indispensable to the search for truth.

Women should learn to disagree without being emotional about it, and the wise teacher will recognize that it's ridiculous to be dogmatic on debatable questions. Students (and faculty) should learn to respect opinions that differ from their own, and sometimes it's a good idea for students in the Catholic women's college to take a summer session at another type of institution. This will do two things for them if they are intelligent and thoughtful: it will make them appreciate the excellence of their college and give them a kind of yardstick to measure the worth of their education. The ability to take their places in a larger group without undue strain should increase their respect for the small women's college.

But if women need men socially and intellectually, they also need them economically. Whatever statistics may have to say about the seventy-odd per cent of the national wealth controlled by women, I can only conclude that we must have enrolled the other thirty per cent, and financial problems loom large on our horizon.

Holy Names College is owned and operated by the Society of the Sisters of the Holy Names of Jesus and Mary. Although all the Sisters are Roman Catholics, that's about the extent of the church-relatedness. Holy Names receives no direct church support of any kind, and it would probably go out of business tomorrow if the American economy were not built so completely on the loan system. Its operating budget early in the decade was $232,000, plus another $180,000 in contributed services from the faculty. Tuition accounted for about seventy per cent of its income, with the other thirty per cent divided among gifts, grants, alumnae contributions, endowment interest and auxiliary enterprises.

The president and other college administrators are appointed by the provincial superior and her council, who act as trustees for the college. For more than a decade, Holy Names College has had a board of regents, composed of lay men and women, who serve in an advisory capacity, largely in matters of finance. Although there must be many corporation executives who serve on similar boards without benefit of salary, it requires heroic dedication to give one's time without benefit of authority. Unlike the Sisters, the regents are not bound by a vow of obedience, and their willingness to work with and for us in the midst of the elaborate system of checks and balances that constitutes a religious community is one of the miracles of our daily existence.

The building program that first gave Holy Names College an independent existence was made possible by a fund-raising campaign led by Frank S. McWilliams, president of Spokane's Fidelity Savings & Loan Association, later first chairman of the board. One of a long line of laymen to serve without any recompense but the growth of the College and the gratitude of the Sisters, he typified the ideals of faith and service that make up our permanent endowment.

Any complete listing of our assets would have to take account of something else that makes the contributed service of the faculty doubly effective. I refer to the goals that impel the Sister-teacher—the things we want to do as works of mercy. My own list was long and growing every day.

I wanted to share with alert and eager young women the insights that literature can provide. I wanted to clear away the obstacles so that they could discover the incredible power of poetry to say the unsayable. I wanted to let them know that they did not need to be afraid of life; that they could live deeply and purposefully with a minimum of external comforts; that their inner resources were more important than economic status or social prestige; above all that the best things in life *are* free to those who have learned by love to penetrate beneath the surface.

I knew that, old-fashioned as it sometimes sounds, woman is the heart of the home, and I wanted more and more students to be transformed with the spiritual energy that makes a family something more convincing than a magazine advertisement for togetherness.

I wanted to help every student to realize her full potential: to inculcate a sense of responsibility for the gifts of mind and body imparted to each. Creativity in whatever form is an act of love, and love is diffusive of itself. So I wanted them to bring the joy of their creativity into sorrowing corners of the world; the light of their perceptions into the alien darkness; and the strength of their confident faith into the desolate wastes of unbelief. I wanted them to know that all men are brothers and that love implies more than mere giving. It is an unselfish exchange and involves "being done unto" as well as doing; implies receiving from other cultures, not always imposing our own.

I knew that my own part in the history of the human race was microscopic, but joined to the total work, it took on an importance not to be lightly discounted. To gain the whole world for Christ is essentially a missionary idea, but there is something of the missionary in every Sister, and an extra large portion in the poet, who is seldom daunted for long by mere practicalities.

CHAPTER III

I had been at the College long enough to see three presidents grapple with mounting debts and static enrollment, and I agreed with the corporation executive who said: "We have so many problems that we've stopped calling them that. Now we refer to them as challenges."

We were probably the most challenged faculty in the whole U.S.A. Both our assignments and our physical plant were like the knight who jumped on his horse and rode off in all directions. I used to wonder how much administrative genius or money it would take for a major improvement and find a gloomy sort of comfort in blaming the challenges on the missing root of all evil. But I felt that there must be something we could do to unify and coordinate our efforts. That we were not making maximum use of our resources, even though individually everybody was working very hard.

I was still one of those who volunteered when "the younger Sisters" were asked to help out with some manual work that didn't come under the regular duties of our hired help. It might be setting up chairs in the gymnasium, which doubled as auditorium, or carrying extra chairs for a well-attended program. It might be dismantling the girls' dining room and preparing it for a reception or tea. The janitor worked an eight-hour shift, but Sisters were on call for twenty-four. In convents women get used to doing many things for themselves that men would handle in an ordinary household. For economic and more mysterious reasons, there seems to be an extraordinary amount of furniture moving in convents. And since the College Sisters normally are transferred less often than elementary and secondary school teachers, the percentage of young recruits is proportionately lower and the practice in juggling beds, tables and pianos more intensive.

Yet I had come to feel at home in this environment where the personnel were more permanent and the properties more mobile. Each year I watched two or three newcomers arrive as I had come to the College faculty: home from the rigors of higher study, eager to resume the teaching apostolate, happy to be back with the community, a bit fearful of the demands of a new assignment, but full of ideas and energy and enthusiasm.

I saw them go through the initial difficulties of readjustment to the common life after an interval of independence, away from the community where they had been free to regulate their own schedule and make their own decisions about many matters which were decided for them at home. They had to learn where to draw the line between the greater autonomy necessarily permitted to college faculty members and the life of obedience exacted of all religious.

They soon realized that the students were quick to discover the stronger areas of the curriculum and that department heads had to develop sound, long-range programs to attract majors. Often, extracurricular demands added to their class loads proved burdensome, and they began to wonder how one person could make a dent in the mountain of things to be done. It was like being called in to construct a building and then being told that they must first dig the clay and bake the bricks or fell the trees and saw the lumber.

I understood their sense of helplessness when they first bumped painfully against the limits of their own physical endurance and realized that not even the hardiest good will could forever stave off fatigue. I prayed for and with them as they learned the relaxed grip: the goal centered in, and subordinate in all things to the Will of God. Without giving way to defeatism, they gradually cultivated detachment from visible and tangible results. They worked just as hard, but not so feverishly; and out of their growing serenity, fed by deep springs of faith and fervor under the superficial dryness, there burst a torrent of inexhaustible trust.

For many it was a lonely pilgrimage. In fact, one might almost say that loneliness was its indispensable concomitant. One does not journey through the desert in a fleet of luxury liners; nor up the heights of Everest on an elevated railway. Neither does one learn to place all his confidence in God by having his slightest personal effort crowned with instant success.

Life at the College differed from that in the smaller convents attached to parochial schools. There, everybody knew at any minute of the day what all the other Sisters were doing. Table conversation turned on topics understood by everyone and shared in a close, personal way.

The College faculty members had common interests, too, but departmental lines were boldly drawn, and it took a while before an art teacher could show Sisterly concern about the antiquated typewriters in the secretarial department; or a philosopher could make allowance for the imprecisions and the deadline pressures of the journalist. Each Sister was responsible for the functioning of an independent unit—sometimes for several—and at first it was hard not to feel like a hermit.

Time had a way of winning the doubters, though, and the sure sign of complete conversion was the spirited defense an old-timer would raise in answer to a recent recruit who wanted to know whether the whole thing was worth the trouble. I remember how I surprised myself by publishing the praises of a colleague whose professional ability I had once questioned and whose unassuming competence had subsequently won my regard. I had learned to gauge the strength of my Sisters more accurately, and I appreciated the unspoken loyalties and the deeply personal sincerity that joined forty-two individualists in a unity that nobody recognized as unity until it was threatened from without.

For example, there was Sister Clotilde, head of the education department. Everybody in the Inland Empire and lots of others beyond it recognized her professional contributions. Those who knew her better wondered how she managed such an output of energy against the odds of ill health and frequent accident. She walked mainly on will power, for her feet were often more of a handicap than a help, and she was capable of getting right up out of a hospital bed and flying into a work routine that would (and frequently did) stagger an able-bodied man.

In Sister Clotilde's view, the mere fact that a thing was impossible seemed insufficient grounds for giving up. She had started work on the doctorate during a period of "convalescence" and had completed it during summers and after hours. Confronted, as all small college faculty members are, with inadequate opportunity to discuss her field with others, she refused to abandon professional progress. Through independent reading, through participation in professional meetings, through research and writing, through summer courses and unappeasable curiosity, she stayed alive intellectually.

I remember seeing a prayer that goes something like this: "Dear Lord, give us the energy and determination to change the things we can, the grace to accept the things we can't, and the wisdom to know the difference." Whenever there was any doubt about the difference, Sister Clotilde was on the side of energy and determination.

For years she had been looking for a millionaire philanthropist, because it was obvious that we needed money. But in the meantime, she went right ahead meeting the academic problems head-on, and the number of students majoring in education reflected her dynamic leadership as much as the College's origins in a two-year normal school.

Not everyone could match Sister Clotilde's moral stamina. Some of us found it harder to cope with a lack of professional stimulation, with the burden of extracurricular activities, and with an enrollment that grew too slowly for our ambitions.

Certain basic expenditures of money and time would be the same for five hundred students as for two hundred. Overhead, library, faculty salaries would remain about the same, even if our student body doubled. And you didn't really work much harder, though often more effectively, teaching ten or fifteen students than teaching three.

Like the freshman who wanted to know what book he could read to become liberally educated, I longed for a shatterproof priority list for my time and talent. Sometimes I thought that what I needed most was the chance to get outside the situation and take a long look. But much of the time I felt like an artillery man trying to read the instruction manual while under enemy fire.

In a civilization where higher education was becoming more and more necessary the old patterns were shifting. The percentage of students educated in private colleges dropped as the cost of tuition mounted, and though the American college population was growing rapidly, we seemed not to get a proportionate share of the increase. What was the reason?

Part of it was monetary. For a time our tuition had been kept much too low on the theory that our students were drawn from an economically underprivileged group. But as students transferred from Holy Names to more expensive colleges, we began to realize that the low price we put on our program was unflattering. In a relatively short time we nearly doubled our tuition. This brought the figure into more reasonable relation with operating costs; made it comparable to the charge at Marylhurst, our Oregon college; and partially closed the gap between our tuition and Gonzaga's.

Scholarships continued to pose a question. The idea prevails today that anybody with better than average ability ought to have a scholarship, whether or not he needs one. Many of our students did. Eventually we made use of scientific services to determine need, but we felt that good students could make a contribution to the College, so we continued to hold out some inducements to the highly qualified and to those talented in music and art.

One music scholarship student, from a small town where the English language is preserved in a more distinctive form, was told to write a thank-you letter to the donor of her scholarship. "Dear Miss X," she began. "I am the girl you made possible to study music at Holy Names College. . . ."

It did seem at times that we were expected to produce students by some sleight-of-hand process not yet discovered. Yet it was hard to believe that women in the Pacific Northwest were so different from women elsewhere that they wouldn't go to a college unless it was coeducational. Statistics do show that the percentage who choose a women's college is relatively low, but we thought that students would come if the College were good enough.

The physical plant, crowded as it was, seemed even more scattered than the Sisters' energies. Our multi-purpose faculty pursued their multiform common goal in a whole series of multipurpose rooms.

The "Green Room" vied with the gym in the number of its uses. It was the resident students' dining room, furnished with folding tables that could be removed for teas and receptions and for lectures and meetings limited to one hundred. Chemistry classes often moved in to take examinations. Music students practiced voice or piano. Faculty members paused for a few minutes' study or to confer with students. Drama groups found refuge here when the gym was in use by some other clientele.

The music department had spread out in several directions—all of them distractingly audible. In the administration building vocal exercises floated through the thin partition separating the department from the president's office, and out the windows to the labs and classrooms above. Backstage in the gym, more practice rooms sent musical charms across to the Sisters' chapel and up to the journalism room or onstage to the play cast or drama class. I had never really learned to appreciate the piano, though, until they moved an electric organ into the small room below my combination office, staff room and classroom. Whenever they wanted the organ on stage for a recital or College function, they had to take the door off its hinges and remove the casing to widen the opening to get the organ out again.

If I wearied of aesthetic pleasures, there was always basketball. Instead of vibrating with the organ that rattled radiators in my office, I could follow a game by the thud of the basketball downstairs and the cheering, stamping mob of high school girls who watched it. When I wrote my first book, some publicity man wanted to know, "Must you have quiet when you write?"

The art department had overflowed its original quarters on the top floor of the administration building to two basement rooms in Marian Hall, where work areas remained at a premium. Here, as in science classes, students learned to accommodate their gestures to limited space like actors confining their stage movements for the television camera. The original art room doubled as gallery and studio for painting and design without being big enough for either. Exhibits, less disciplined than students, dribbled out the door and down the hallway to create one more hazard at class breaks.

When the intermission bell rang the long narrow halls looked narrower still, and making your way from one end to the other called for expert dodging. Doors opened outward into the hall, and students dragged chairs or desks from room to room for some of the required courses. It was like one of those picturesque streets in Chicago where everything available in the stores is displayed on the sidewalk.

The language department had installed a laboratory in the living room of a faculty house across from the administration building.

But perhaps the most acute space shortage was in our chapel. To those who believe in the Real Presence of Our Lord in the Blessed Sacrament, the sanctuary is the center of the campus. From it radiates the Divine Strength and Wisdom that are the only real explanation of the energies at work in the Catholic college. The Sisters spend about three hours daily in spiritual exercises of Rule, and the students gather there for such formal occasions as the Mass of the Holy Spirit to invoke God's blessing on the college year. Yet our chapel could accommodate only fifteen per cent of our students.

Built originally for eighteen or twenty Sisters, its capacity had been doubled by removing the sliding doors and annexing the community room. This had the effect of destroying the original architecture, as the room had to be turned around, so that the organ, not the altar, occupied a recessed focal area. The Sisters could put up with the crowding, but some provision had to be made for the students. We had a portable altar constructed, and moved it into the gymnasium-auditorium-chapel. Aside from the scheduling problem, there was the matter of getting the "chapel" ready. With skill and practice the routine could be reduced to an hour, but it was faculty time taken for details that, in other circumstances, might have been delegated to unskilled labor.

The library had long since become too small to contain either our collection of books or the people who wanted to read them. Once it was filled, the only other places for students to go were the smoker or the cafeteria. Since neither was a place of silence, concentration suffered.

Our campus store, tucked into an extension of the stair landing between the ground and the main floor, dispensed books, stationery, school supplies and anything else the proprietor was ingenious enough to find room for. We finally had to turn the job over to a mathematician because she was the only one who could figure out how to get everything in. Or how to unpack the textbooks without falling out the window.

The clothing laboratory on the ground floor of the College had very little daylight and inadequate artificial light.

Chemistry and foods laboratories, also located on this floor, had similar problems.

The obvious solution for the crowding would seem to be more building, but the longer we looked at our plant, the more we wondered about its location.

We were too close to our own high school students and shared our gymnasium with them. This proximity subtracted from the glamor of "going away to college." Being near Gonzaga had its advantages, but people persisted in regarding us as an annex. Our president had once received a letter addressed to Gonzaga College of the Holy Names. Our women's residence, Marian Hall, was often confused with Gonzaga's dormitory, Madonna Hall. And one fond mother had written a touching message, confiding her Gonzaga daughter to the care of "the good Sisters." Besides, the blessings of coeducation looked irresistible at that range. But perhaps the major disadvantage was having so little room to grow.

A wide weeded area (the vowels were important) separated us from the railroad track. And since boxcars seemed a permanent part of that landscape, one of the Sisters always volunteered to call the Great Northern and ask to have them removed when we had planned any special event, especially if it were out of doors.

Officials usually cooperated, but the boxcars always came back, vocal with sheep, and the trains rattled through my late-morning lecture, forcing me to consider taking up sign language. It was useless to compete with a diesel engine, but I never stopped trying because it always seemed to me that the commerce in ideas had right-of-way over that in commodities.

From these same boxcars, a procession of vagrants wandered up to our kitchen door looking for handouts and mounted the fire escape to "The Deck," a second-floor porch next to the cloister bedrooms. At first we gave the men food, but neighbors complained that this kept them around and endangered children. So, at the request of city officials, we began sending the hungry to social agencies. One soggy morning a Sister discovered a pair of trousered legs protruding from the shelter of a low toolhouse near the garden, where a stranger had evidently spent the night. It was not unusual to meet an obviously displaced person roaming the halls of the administration building. Such experiences made it seem unwise to build a dormitory in this area, even if the occupants could put up with the noise. Instead we began pricing a cyclone fence to run along the border of the bluff overlooking the railroad track.

Of course we could always tell ourselves that students don't go to college for the buildings or the campus. In a way it was true. But down the street Gonzaga's expansion program moved ahead while we waited and prayed and tried to scrape together enough to meet the interest payments on our loans.

Sister Clotilde insisted that we had to develop a first-rate fund-raising program. She cited numerous predictions regarding the demise of all but the best of the women's colleges and concluded with dry irony that we had a few things to do before we insured our continuity.

So we went on, year after year, always a little deeper in debt, always planning new miracles that God might perform for us if we prayed and worked just a fraction harder than we had done hitherto. There were friends who helped us out occasionally, as generously as their means allowed, but there were others who sent large gifts elsewhere and the old attic furniture to us. We had to admit that it looked like the scriptural, ". . . to everyone that hath shall be given . . ." for the few legacies and bequests that came our way seemed minor compared with the liberal gifts regularly made to other institutions in our area.

We rationalized, of course. Our alumnae association was young. Most of our graduates were still pinching pennies to feed and clothe five or six children. Some day we'd put our mortarboard on a feminine counterpart of Bing Crosby, and our worries would be over—almost.

But in the meantime, to stave off the flood of bankruptcy, daily made more real by the closing down of other colleges, we continued with the usual card parties and rummage sales and luncheons and style shows. Sometimes it seemed like trying to pave a coast-to-coast freeway with a plastic bag full of kindergarten clay.

CHAPTER IV

Sister Superior sat on the edge of her swivel chair in the president's office at Holy Names College sorting the morning mail. Seven piles rose up in front of her, and a larger, less disposable one sprawled at her left elbow. A gentle Spokane breeze rattled the venetian blind pleasantly from time to time, and sunlight glanced off the yellow walls or struck reflections from the waxed turquoise inset in the Formica-topped desk. Every now and then she flipped a letter into the wrong pile, and, pausing to retrieve it, placed it elsewhere before dealing out the rest.

Behind her on the credenza, *The Canterbury Tales* and *The Divine Comedy* rubbed bindings with the poems of Gerard Manley Hopkins and the current issue of *Sewanee Review*, constant symbols of the world from which she came and to which she hoped one day to escape. It was a serene hope, though, unmarred by the wracking violence that troubled smaller natures like my own, and it came out in sunny colloquialisms like: "I can't wait to get rid of this job and go back to my medieval romance with sophomores and world literature."

Off to one side the secretary presided at a similar ritual for second- and third-class mail. The cabinet on which she worked was not large enough, even with baskets for incoming and outgoing letters removed, so Sister kept shift-

ing the dean's envelopes to the bottom of the stack as she
sorted. She found two pieces addressed to the president,
carried them over to Sister Superior's desk, and, standing
politely back, waited until the last piece of first-class had
been tossed into a pile. Then she raised her eyebrows ex-
pectantly as Sister Superior pulled out a wastebasket and
began dealing with the correspondence addressed to Sister
Michael Mary, President.

Grey eyes gleamed behind thick glasses, badge of the
lifelong reader, and a smile, direct and impartial as sun-
shine, let people know that she remembered all the details
of the human comedy and found them singly dear.

"Nothing today," Sister Superior said, as I moved in
from the doorway where I had been hovering. All three
of us knew that *nothing* meant nothing except the usual
bills and business correspondence. A friendly check for
five thousand dollars, a foundation grant or a corporation
gift to the independent colleges would have been something.

"Maybe tomorrow," Sister Superior said. "It's Wednes-
day. St. Joseph's day." As provider for the Holy Family,
St. Joseph was supposed to look after all our financial
needs. It occurred to me that his hands must be full just
taking care of us, and I wondered whether we ought to
give up and spend our energies in more rewarding territory. Genuine need had called the College into existence,
but perhaps its days of usefulness were over now.

Although Holy Names College had a brief history, as
colleges go, it grew from a century-old tradition. The Sisters of the Holy Names of Jesus and Mary had come to

Portland in 1859, the year Oregon became a state. The community's educational record in the Pacific Northwest had been the story of the region's academic needs. St. Mary's Academy, our first Oregon school, was established at a time when there was little opportunity for girls to get a Catholic education. Day schools and boarding schools sprang up in the various centers as the population grew. Parish schools, elementary and secondary, often were coeducational when no other facilities existed for boys. And along with these, normal schools were opened with curricula gradually extended as the state lengthened the period of preparation for teachers. At the time when we started our normal school in Spokane in 1907 there was no other Catholic higher institution for women in the city. Even in 1940 Gonzaga was strictly for men, and we were lengthening the period of higher education in line with current trends. So the College had begun in answer to a public need, though it was to our advantage to have a community-owned-and-operated college to educate our own Sisters at the undergraduate level.

"Washington's Only Women's College" we called ourselves, stressing a distinction no one seemed to covet. The trend of the times was against us. As Catholic universities for men went co-ed all around us, we listened to gloomy prophecies about the future of the women's colleges and wondered whether ours would be among the survivors. The whole situation sometimes made me feel as if I were teaching my classes atop an iceberg that had drifted down into temperate waters: I kept right on going through the usual motions, but I sometimes had a sinking feeling not wholly divorced from reality. Higher education was becoming more and more expensive, and many private colleges were pricing themselves out of the market.

To some observers, we must have seemed like the ostrich; to others, like Noe, bargaining with God for the survival of a few favored souls. When we had to talk of our enrollment we said it was "about two hundred" with a vagueness born of indefinite hope; and, like Noe, we argued earnestly with reluctant superiors who sometimes wondered whether we should give up the struggle at Holy Names and concentrate on staffing and building up a single strong college in the Oregon Province. Marylhurst College near Portland, Oregon, established in 1930, had replaced St. Mary's College, chartered in 1893 with St. Mary's Academy. Located on the same campus with our novitiate, Marylhurst was dear to every Sister in the Oregon Province, but Holy Names College was a stepsister.

Demands for more teachers in elementary and secondary schools were growing every year. When we had about fifty schools to staff, the thought of Sisters teaching small college classes while grade school teachers handled classes of fifty or more all day long seemed incongruous.

We wondered sometimes whether our own Sisters believed in Holy Names College. They'd let something slip about hoping their students or their nieces would go to Marylhurst, and then there would be an embarrassing pause before they added, "or to Holy Names." It seemed to us that we ought to get more graduates from Holy Names high schools if our own Sisters were proud of us.

Of course the picture couldn't be unrelieved black, and I tried to assess the whole more objectively than college catalogs usually do.

After twenty years as an independent four-year college, our claim to liberal arts status was still shaky. As many as two-thirds of some graduating classes were education majors, and Sister Clotilde had been so successful with that department that placement was no problem. We had established a solid reputation for excellence in art and music, and from small beginnings, other departments showed signs of strength: social science, foreign languages, biology, English, home economics. Our faculty members were making contributions in scholarly and creative activities, and the College had brought to the local community important cultural and educational opportunities.

But in an era that makes so much of numbers, it's hard not to be influenced by purely quantitative measurement. When everyone around you is talking about the mobs beating for admission upon college doors, you begin to suspect that something is amiss if you are still out beating the bushes to coax them in. Have you, then, no real function to serve in higher education? Is your college so limited and inferior that you'd have trouble giving it away? Should you, in justice to the student, give up the struggle?

In a follow-up interview on his resounding criticism of American Catholics and the intellectual life, Monsignor John Tracy Ellis of the Catholic University of America repeated his ideas on the proliferation of Catholic colleges and the duplication of facilities. He deplored the lack of long-range planning and recommended a national planning board with ten or twelve leaders of American Catholic education representing as many elements as possible.

Monsignor Ellis' suggestions were thoughtful and well-timed. It made me wince when he said that the real reason for duplication of offerings was not a wealth of resources but institutional pride. And he indicated that the threat of bankruptcy might force a reform.

Maybe cooperation was the answer. The principal difficulty seemed to lie in the *co*. It was more likely to be just plain operation—major surgery that would lop off the torso of our effort and leave a few disconnected limbs like the music department and the women's dormitories.

In Oklahoma a Catholic women's college closed down and we borrowed one of its Ph.D's for our history department. In Salt Lake City, Utah's only women's college collapsed quietly and we picked up a couple of students. In Spokane, Seattle and Portland, universities for men, recently made coeducational, drew more and more women, while our applications dribbled in and the bills came at the usual lively rate.

Some of the faculty thought of easy solutions. All we had to do was change the name of the College, and the whole wide world would suddenly know that we were not a high school ("That's Holy Names *Academy*"), not a finishing school ("Oh, do you teach history at Holy Names?"), not a novitiate ("You mean regular girls go here?"), but a college. They talked euphemistically about "preserving our identity" while I pondered the headmaster's verdict in "The Fifty-First Dragon": "You're *nobody*. You can't be more invisible than that."

I hoped that we were not being merely stubborn. I mulled over a few ideas from the 1960 *Official Guide to Catholic Educational Institutions*. "Catholic men's colleges, in strength and solid organization, preceded women's colleges." But it looked as if the women's colleges had more "staying power." During the worst depression years women religious had established twenty-nine colleges, and all but one were still operating in the early 1960s. In the same time period men religious established eight, four of which no longer exist. The growth of the Sisters' colleges was traceable in part to their own professional growth and their newly-acquired experience in organizing curricula. Cooperation among the various orders helped the Sisters to develop programs for the undergraduate education of their own Sisters, and mutual support and encouragement toward graduate study received an impetus from Pope Pius XII's address to the first international Congress of Teaching Sisters.

In that 1951 address, the Holy Father indicated that parents who send their daughters to the Sisters' schools must not be penalized by having them receive an inferior education. He urged that the professional preparation of the Sisters equal or surpass that of their lay counterparts.

I could see how the College enriched the lives of all our Sisters—not just those who were on the faculty or in attendance there. Sisters from the entire city profited by the programs and lectures the College sponsored. Sisters in schools outside the city shared in the intellectual life in a less direct way, but nonetheless really. The ideal of the Sister-scholar or the Sister-intellectual, as a leader in the Sister-Formation program had pointed out, was essentially a *community* endeavor.

But if the need to educate our own Sisters was to justify the existence of Holy Names College, the College had to be twice as good. For here and at Marylhurst we were preparing those who would teach more than 19,000 students in Oregon and Washington at all levels from kindergarten to college. The Sisters went elsewhere for graduate study, but their success in working toward advanced degrees depended in part on their previous education. Were we equal to the challenge?

Mere attachment to the College was not enough. Perhaps long association had dulled my critical powers. During my years on the faculty I had grown to love every brick in the administration building. I had followed Marian Hall from the ground-breaking right through the open house and the invasion of each year's crop of homesick newcomers, who changed, if they weathered the first difficult weeks, into excitable freshmen and then into confident sophomores, ready to console their "little sisters" the next time around.

My feet knew in the dark exactly how many steps led upward, beyond the swinging door in the gymnasium, to the press room where I taught and worked. I could tell by a glance at their faces when Sister Phillip, who sat beside me at table, had begun a new sculpture, and whether Sister Superior had decided to write her own speech, turn over her notes to her secretary, or enlist me as a ghostwriter.

It was quite possible that my image of the College was

identical with that of its president and superior. My loyalty to Holy Names might be merely an extension of my loyalty to her. During my first year in Spokane we had been assigned to Loretto Hall, where about twenty residents lived. It was an old house, but the girls liked it for its homey atmosphere and relaxed, informal discipline. Besides dormitory duties, we shared an enthusiasm for poetry, which we tried to write occasionally; an interest in improving our teaching of English (Sister was department head, and I had a class in freshman English). We shared, besides, a small bedroom on the second floor. Since we took turns staying up until the students retired or came in from late leaves, we managed to wake each other up on alternate nights. This lasted only until Christmas time, when I was judged not strong enough to continue such a schedule, and somebody else took my place in the dormitory. Five years later my department chairman was my superior—and president.

When one of your friends suddenly becomes your superior, you lose and you gain at the same time. You lose because she will from then on be hedged about with the cares and confidences of the entire community. She will stand on a solitary eminence between earth and heaven, marked by the divine seal of the cross in the eternal mystery of the suffering Christ. But you will gain immeasurably, too, for in being made your superior, your friend becomes for you "the sacrament of the Will of God," and you are bound to her by an intimate, personal and mutually sanctifying relationship.

You will never again be so free in your dealings with

her, for you must consider whether you are contriving to use your friendship to gain your own will. At the same time, your love will prompt you to ease the burden of her office by the most generous offering you can make of your time and abilities. Yet in all this, you must learn to keep your heart free; to work first of all for God, Who asks an undivided service, and to make no more than the necessary claims on the superior's time and attention.

Every fall when the newspaper called to check on our enrollment, somebody was sure to ask, "When is Holy Names going co-ed?" There were various answers to the question, ranging from a tone of light banter to one of bleak despair.

We had admitted a few men to individual classes in art, music and home economics but these students were clearly labeled exceptions, for we had no serious thought of altering our educational policy.

Every year two Gonzaga men lived at Holy Names College and worked for their room and board. We used to call them our Holy Names Boys, and they must have put up with a certain amount of good-natured teasing from their fellow students. But they polished a few apples as they cleaned classrooms, and soon our chemistry teacher was coaching them outside class hours, or our librarian was finding research materials for them, or our English teachers were helping them with special problems.

Out of this reciprocal arrangement with Gonzaga grew a number of Gonzaga-Holy Names alliances, and there began a steady procession of returning couples: Joe and Margie, Steve and Darlene, Norman and Loretta.

One year we had two Chinese boys, Jack and Mike. When they finished at Gonzaga, our Holy Names Placement Service reached down into our California Province and found them a similar job at one of our high schools there, where they worked while attending graduate school.

It was the little human things like these that made the College worth saving, but the human factor seemed to be fast disappearing from the higher educational scene. Mark Hopkins' famous log with a student at one end and a teacher at the other was out of date. Repeatedly, newspaper stories omitted any mention of Holy Names College, and when the omission was called to editorial attention, the reason always seemed connected with size, and we started all over again to wonder whether the judgment of numbers was not conclusive in our doom.

I had come here with a few doubts myself. But now the College had somehow merged with the city and the region and my life, and I did not know whether I could ever separate the parts again.

I watched the seasons turn with the row of maple trees along our front parking, where my eyes had learned to measure the interval between January's black branches and the first slow traces of green that kept their secret through a long cold April and then leafed out delicately as blossoms, in a color and texture that justified the delay.

My first few years in the Inland Empire, I missed the early springs I had known on the Pacific Coast. A trip in March to Portland or Seattle, where I'd find camellias in blossom and orchards showing pink, would send me back to Spokane impatient with the sun.

But in time I came to believe that the very profusion of leaf and flower in the coastal region desensitized the observer. I learned to enjoy each distinct stage in natural growth in Spokane where an all but imperceptible color change in the strings of the weeping willow foretold the spring. It was not unusual, even after magnolia flowered, to walk out into a biting wind that scattered the huge petals across a reviving lawn.

There were besides the intricacies of light, and I had learned to know and love them all: the extraordinary clarity of May; the blinding brilliance of July; the crisp transparence of October, merging into November's mellow haze; the subdued, shadowy light of a February.

If changing our name or going co-ed wouldn't work, maybe we ought to look for another solution—moving the College, for instance.

The Sisters with vision had canvassed the city for a new campus and had come home with several likely suggestions. Mother Cabrini style, one of them had even made an appointment with a multimillionaire who might like to give us a section of choice property. But everybody realized that an open-air college on the ancient Greek plan was out of the question in our harsh winters, even if the Chamber of Commerce did call Spokane the Athens of the Inland Empire. We'd have to ask for a pair of miracles, since property alone wouldn't do the trick. Our California college had sold its downtown site to Kaiser Aluminum for 2½ million dollars and had built a complete new plant on Mountain Boulevard. Enrollment was growing steadily there.

But nobody would pay enough for our property to build a new campus, and even logs were more expensive than in Hopkins' time. Then somebody else came up with a really outlandish idea: why not move to Fort George Wright? The thousand-acre tract was declared surplus to the needs of the Strategic Air Command, and if no other federal agency claimed it, the land would be made available for private development. Educational institutions were to have priority in the disposal, and somebody suggested that the government might give us a campus. This was the kind of improbable scheme that always appealed to us, for what was the point in escaping from tedious reality to a world only slightly less pale than the one we'd left? No, better to reach for the moon.

I had no trouble at all in fitting this idea into the collection I'd amassed over the years. We were also, at various times, going to: sell film rights to one of the Sisters' books; graduate an heiress and stumble into an endowment; win the Irish Sweepstakes and build a chapel.

American Sisters get the wildest ideas and then calmly stand by, marking time with their rosaries, and waiting for the universe to adjust. Moving the U.S. government would be quite an undertaking, especially at such a distance from Capitol Hill. As Sister Clotilde observed, the notion was utterly impossible, unthinkable, inconceivable.

So we ought to send in our application right away.

CHAPTER V

Sister Superior had clipped the original newspaper story, the way a housewife might clip an advertisement for cut-rate potatoes at the neighborhood grocery, and had tucked it into the top drawer of her desk. Each time a faculty member came into the office, she'd pull out the clipping and ask, "How would you like to move the College out to Fort Wright?"

I thought that she might as well say, "How would you like to be the first Sister of the Holy Names in Outer Space?" But I had to admit that it was an exciting new topic for table conversation. The revolutionary age we live in has had its effects even on the conservatism of convent life, and we might as well think about a whole new plant outside the city limits instead of adding a wing to our present administration building and another story to our dormitory. About the only way we had room to expand was up, and that seemed foolish for a college in a non-metropolitan area.

Fort George Wright was a 1,022-acre track about 3½ miles west of city center. It had been given to the federal government by the people of Spokane in 1894 for the establishment of a military post to protect residents from hostile Indians. Originally an infantry post, the fort was taken over by the Second Air Force at the outbreak of

World War II and subsequently served as a housing project for air force personnel, and headquarters for air national guard, army reserve and civil air patrol units.

Before the property could be made available for private use, it had to be cleared through the Department of Defense, and nobody knew how long that would take.

We watched the newspapers for further word and when city officials called for a meeting of all interested parties, Holy Names College sent a representative to declare our intention of applying for a portion of the land.

What had seemed like an absolutely original and daring idea to us had also occurred to twenty other candidates, including the original donor, the City of Spokane. There didn't seem to be much hope, but at this point we had little to lose, so we kept a hand in the game. We were not alone in our class. Other educational institutions expressing an interest in the property included Eastern Washington College of Education, Gonzaga University, Whitworth, the Lutheran School Board, Washington State University, School District 81, and the University of Washington. Together, they served a total of more than 58,000 students—a formidable array against which to match our "about two hundred." EWCE, Gonzaga and Whitworth withdrew early, leaving us to wonder whether they agreed with former mayor Arthur Meehan that the property would only be a white elephant.

The Boy Scouts wanted the Officers' Club. The Historical Society wanted a museum, and so did the Indians. The Park Board wanted more land along the river bank. Other proposals favored state office buildings or fish and wildlife refuges. Some citizens wanted a community college; others, mental health facilities. Some of the land was almost sure to go for residential purposes, and a Seattle group wanted to buy part of the property. Those were the conditions under which we were "bidding" for eighty-five acres.

Even before we saw the property, many of our own faculty members were collecting objections. They always managed to find the most colorful headlines and place them conspicuously in the telephone room where they might be effective instruments in molding opinion. You might walk in for your turn at portress duty and find

MANY BOOST FORT WRIGHT AS CEMETERY

and then you'd be left to reflect on the future of Holy Names College in *that* setup. Or you'd come in after a style show or a tea, your memory stored with those trim figures and fresh young faces, and discover

ALCOHOLICS UNIT EYED FOR BASE

It was a big piece of property, of course, and there would be room for many groups. But who would your neighbors be? Would a gravel pit be a pleasant exchange for a railroad track? Or mental patients better company than orphans?

Quite apart from your own faculty, there was the question of public opinion. Would church-state tensions be aroused too much if we succeeded in getting part of the land?

We couldn't talk forever about a place we'd seen only

in passing, so we went out to look over the fort. Our advance guard had assured us that we would not like what we saw. Fort Wright was outside the city limits. It enjoyed no bus service, no adequate fire and police protection, no neighborhood shopping center. The buildings were more than sixty years old. The whole place was run down. The upkeep alone would be staggering. We ought to stay where we belonged, the critics said, and hold on to a good thing when we had it.

But we wanted to see for ourselves. So I called the sergeant and asked if he could take us through some of the buildings.

Sister Edward agreed to drive. She maneuvered The Jewel, our ancient Plymouth handed down by a friend who had stopped driving, with the ease of one brought up on stick shifts and uneven country roads. It was a snub-nosed green car, built high like many models of the thirties, and it seated five comfortably.

I watched her bare hands on the steering wheel. They were big and shapeless like a pair of garden gloves, and it was hard to remember them moving expertly over cello strings, charming rich tones from that mellow instrument as Sister Edward played in concert or gave a lesson to one of the students.

"Fine arts in the front seat," I thought, for Sister Phillip was beside her, looking as usual as if she had just emerged from a spray-paint job in an auto refinishing plant.

Sister Phillip and Sister Edward were mountain-movers. Literally, as well as metaphorically. They often went on expeditions to neighboring clay pits and came home with gunnysacks full of yellow or reddish earth, which Sister Phillip's artistic eye and their combined energies would transform into something decorative or useful. No job ever seemed too big for them, and I knew before we started that they would be one hundred per cent for the fort no matter what we might see there. To them, it represented space and challenge—a place to keep the logs and tiles and colored glass they would turn into objects of beauty. As for the difficulties that might lie between us and a new campus, they would shrug their shoulders and remind you that the fort, like the tree roots and the disfigured rocks they dragged home, "had possibilities."

We drove across a narrow bridge and through a gate with a huge sign reading George Wright Air Force Base. Our car wound through clusters of ugly barracks, looking shabby and deserted in the grey November drizzle. We drove on past several monstrous brick buildings, their windows broken or boarded over, and onto The Circle, where officers from Fairchild Air Force Base still lived. Weeds had overgrown the brick walks connecting vacant houses, and the lawns in all but a few places were brown with neglect.

Mentally, I tried to calculate the quantity of road-clearing and lawn-mowing and night watching required to maintain a place like this—or even a small part of it. I thought of our harassed custodian rushing from a cafeteria waxing job to the faculty house furnace and knew that he'd never be able to face the fort.

I looked at the towering flagpole, empty as everything else in this forsaken landscape, and thought of Iwo Jima.

"The Marines have landed," I muttered to myself. But I felt no dramatic surge of loyalty and pride, no compelling need to raise aloft my country's flag, but only a great and terrible unwillingness to take up the burden of this cross.

"We can have commencement right out there on the parade ground," Sister Edward said. "An acoustic shell over to the left would take care of the singing."

I could see the program, all neatly arranged in her mind, complete with orchestral numbers and an impressive procession. Loudspeakers would be in place, graduates seated on the platform, floral decorations tastefully arranged. We'd be moving chairs for a week, I supposed, no doubt borrowing from Gonzaga Prep and the Knights of Columbus. Sister Edward would probably bring several loads in the pickup as if it were a routine she went through every morning like brushing her teeth or picking up the car keys before a trip to town.

Beside me in the back seat, Sister Maria, head of the language department, looked the way I felt. She wasn't saying anything yet, even in French, but I could see her appraising eye on every broken window and sagging porch. She was a mover too, but in a quiet, persistent way that achieved results without any flourish of trumpets or salute of cannons.

Wind veered across the Spokane River and whipped at our habits as we made for the porch of Building 27. We huddled under a huge Off Limits sign as the sergeant fitted a key into the reluctant lock. After a contest of several minutes during which I silently invoked St. Jude, patron of the impossible, the door swung back on its hinges, and we stepped over the fallen plaster and into the building.

Sister Maria lifted her skirts carefully to avoid a pile of rubbish, and Sister Phillip turned over the envelope on which she had been sketching a map of the property and began diagramming the building, estimating room sizes as we went.

Windows had been boarded up in a half-hearted attempt to keep ahead of vandals. Electricity had long since been disconnected, and here and there dead wires hung down from the ceiling or festooned from walls like the parody of a hanging plant. Below them and under some of the sealed windows, pieces of broken glass littered the hardwood floors. Everything detachable seemed to have been detached, and our guide explained that some enterprising collector had been methodically assembling plumbing fixtures and other marketable objects near a fire escape door only to be surprised by the Air Force watch as he was ready to cart them off in a truck. People who were building onto their homes found the nearly deserted post a handy source of supply, the sergeant said, and others must be building their bank balance with profits from second-hand stores.

Children darted in and out of each building opened for our inspection, and the sergeant periodically ordered them out, as they illustrated for us why walk-in freezing compartment doors had been removed and laid on the floor. Everything movable had been removed, and I wondered how we would arrange so necessary a thing as food service.

Surely it would be more costly and more difficult, for the
fort property was extensive, and buildings had not been
planned with a college in mind. Adapting them would
probably be a trial-and-error process complicated by insufficient funds.

Since the mess hall was a temporary building and not
on the ground we thought of asking for, the Base Exchange
(BX) would have to substitute for a dining room. We
would be unwilling to provide cooking and food storage
facilities that would need replacement when the BX became the student union. That is, *if* we got the land and
if we moved, and *if* there ever were need for a student
union and dining room. Always *if*.

Inside the buildings it was colder, with that dank musti-
ness that seeps into closed structures, and we shivered as
we followed the sergeant's flashlight past occasional debris
into the basement where thick cement walls and partially
unpaved floors deepened the darkness.

We were not the only visitors, we learned. Earlier, officers had combed every corner of every building, searching
for Candy Rogers, a child who had disappeared while
selling Camp Fire mints. Police speculated that she or her
captors might be hidden somewhere on the abandoned
base where, in the normal course of events, months might
pass without discovery. The mere suggestion threw a
damper on our adventurousness, and we consistently
stayed near the reassuring beam of light in our group
exploration.

Inside the next building, Sister Maria looked from a
large rent in the plastered ceiling to a treacherous bulge

70

in the battleship linoleum and wanted to know whether I'd like to trade it for Room 303 where I taught world literature.

"That depends," I answered vaguely and gave orders to my face to remain neutral until further notice. Sister Edward had just told Sister Phillip for the third time that she couldn't get over how well-built these old buildings were, and we'd be able to put the whole College in one of them and have room left over.

The third time she said it, we were just entering the attic where some of the windows had been considered high enough for safety and left unboarded. Light leaked onto the recently painted blue walls and the unmistakable evidence that pigeons had taken over this story.

"Attics always make me think of art studios," I said. "Won't the Bohemians love this?"

But Sister Phillip had already agreed with Sister Edward that it would be an excellent place for my journalism classes—so easy to shut out the light and make a darkroom, and there was already running water in that sink in the corner. I bent to avoid cracking my head on the slanted ceiling and hurried toward the stairwell with Sister Maria.

"Now that's one of the better ones," the sergeant said and led the way to Building 25. I looked at Sister Maria out of the corner of my eye and saw her blanch a little. But Sister Edward and Sister Phillip were still talking about the wonderful foundations and the unlimited space.

"Ovah theah," the sergeant said, pointing, "is the mule-bonn. Yawl won't want to bother with that."

"What's a mulebonn?" I asked, eyeing the long, low structure and mentally reviewing BX, GHQ, and NCO Row, newly added to the initialese section of my word hoard.

"A mulebonn," he said with the deadpan look sergeants manage so expertly, "is a place wheah they keep mules."

The sergeant pointed out the jail, which we thought might make a library, and the former library, which he assured us would do for nothing—not even a jail.

"It looks as if somebody went right through the inside of it with a bulldozer," he said.

Building 25 was almost a duplicate of 27 except that it was darker and dirtier and more battered-looking. On the top floor we discovered a barred area.

"Solitary confinement?" Sister Edward wanted to know.

"It may be a padded cell," Sister Maria muttered. "Something like that might be necessary."

But in place of the usual jokes about convent discipline and the dean of women's regulations, I knew that she was contemplating the full horror of the ugliness, the inconvenience, the dirt and disorder. She could not be happy in such a place until she had scrubbed every inch of the walls, floors and woodwork and arranged the rooms as attractively as one could without spending a fortune.

Outside, Sister Maria looked happier. She was evidently visualizing the outdoor prospect in a more kindly season. A hush had fallen over the group, and we got into The Jewel almost forgetting to thank the sergeant for our tour of inspection.

"Let's drive out the other way," Sister Edward suggested, and hearing no objections, she headed the car in that direction.

Paradoxically, the only part of the fort property that showed signs of life was the cemetery. All summer sprinklers had whirred on the pine-bordered grassy plot high on a cliff above the Spokane River. Nearly every day one or another of the small crew tended the well-tailored lawn and locked the gate leading inside the wrought iron fence. From time to time the traditions of a military funeral were carried out here, where the staccato of rifle volleys echoed down the river canyon. Then a bugler sounded the plaintive notes of taps, and pallbearers folded the flag and presented it to the widow.

Judging from the havoc wrought by vandals, the Sisters would have to turn out for guard duty. Not one of our forty-two boasted experience on the rifle range, but the physical education teacher was moderately skillful with bow and arrow—a weapon that might have historic significance in that particular spot, named for a famous fighter of Indians. Once, when a prowler had been lurking around Marian Hall, one of the Sisters had seized her umbrella and rushed out with the look of an avenging Fury to bring the trespasser to task. Told later that her action had been extremely imprudent, she admitted that it was, but her indignation over the threat to the girls overrode her judgment.

I could see it all in imagination: the uniformed Sisters, their white headdress muffled in black winter hoods, patrolling the thin strip of light bordering the duplexes. The chemistry teacher might concoct some sort of tear gas

73

from the bottles in her cupboard, and the voice teacher would sing the Catholic equivalent of "A Mighty Fortress Is Our God." The speech teacher would finally have a practical target for her stentorian challenge and something more interesting to say than, "How now, brown cow?"

Sister Phillip would not be much help. She would only stand and study the pattern of light on the skeleton of the maples and perhaps make a sketch or two. Sister Clotilde would insist on taking her turn, though she would need a bench against the lamp post because of her bad feet. Even so she might be more effective at ease than most sentries at attention.

Sister Superior was sure to wander out unarmed, except with an Office book, and she would linger over Psalm 44 with a gentle smile for its appropriateness. *"Gird Thy sword upon Thy thigh, O most mighty one, Thy glory and Thy adornment!/ Go forth swiftly for faith and justice, and may Thy right hand teach Thee valorous deeds./ Thy arrows are sharp, nations submit to Thee, the enemies of the King lose heart."*

At any rate, the Sisters might fare as well in their unaccustomed occupation as the little nun from Kerala, India, who was offered a ride back to St. Mary's by a Notre Dame professor. When the car got stuck in a snowdrift, the chauffeur realized that Sister couldn't drive while he pushed, so he made the only other possible distribution of duties.

"Would you mind getting out and giving the car a shove?" he asked.

Her tiny figure stationed behind the dark bulk of resistant machinery, the shivering Sister watched the wheels spinning against snow and ice. She made a massive Sign of the Cross and said in her high, clipped syllables, "Je – sus . . . is . . . my . . . STRENGTH!" Then she pushed.

Within seconds there were four men pulling off the high- way to take the little nun in tow.

I made a mental note to remember that technique when the time for it came, and looked out again at the tempo- rary buildings section of the fort.

Back at the College we were instantly surrounded like war heroes at a press conference. The most animated voices—those of Sister Phillip and Sister Edward—set the tone for the whole discussion and, since the sergeant had had the foresight to send us home with a map of the fort, anyone who could not be enthusiastic was free to remain objective. She just pointed on the map to the buildings we had visited, and detailed, with calm neutrality, the ar- rangement and size of the rooms.

Sister Phillip's visual aids and keen sense of direction, added to the artist's photographic memory, gave her re- construction a heightened popularity. Altogether, it was a happy gathering, I thought, and once when I saw Sister Maria smiling quizzically at me while Sister Edward en- larged on the marvellous condition of the buildings, I felt almost like a traitor and looked away.

On the way to chapel for evening prayer, I saw one of the Sisters pause in the arcade and peer into the lighted rectangle outside. She was, I felt sure, admiring the shrub- bery and the lawn which her own careful supervision had brought to their present state of perfection.

"How are the grounds out at the fort?" she wanted to

know, and though I should have said they were terrible, I launched, instead, into an enthusiastic description of the cemetery.

When prayer was over I went to my room for an hour's study. Then I went to bed and dreamed that I was back at the fort. I was presiding over an ingeniously renewed attic, complete with orange-crate bookshelves and cheery cretonne curtains. Everything was lovely except that I was trying hard to mend the windows with Scotch tape, and every time I had the pieces just about in place, a pigeon dive-bombed through the only remaining opening, and I had to begin all over again.

CHAPTER VI

All through the months after that first visit to Fort Wright, Holy Names College looked better to me than it had since the first time I saw it twelve years earlier. It was crowded, yes, but oh so clean and orderly and beautifully kept. Even the refrigerator cars on the railroad tracks seemed less annoying than usual. When I passed Sister Maria getting ready for French class in the kitchen next to the language lab, she looked almost radiant.

The Gonzaga library had suddenly become more important to both of us, and we found ourselves going over every few days for books we couldn't find in our own. We began to wonder how we'd ever manage if we went to the fort and had to trade in our present opportunities for an attic full of Army field manuals.

The marginal notes on our fort inspection trip had now made the rounds of the community, and their effect was evident in altered attitudes. Everywhere you went you'd find small groups of Sisters talking in corners with great shaking of heads and proclaiming of thanks.

We were really well off as things stood. Let me tell you it would take ages at the fort to come to our present luxurious state of living. It was so easy to take for granted necessary things like plumbing and electricity. Why, those old buildings were ready to fall apart. They had a good start already.

And so on. The wind was blowing, and I leaned with it myself a good part of the time. I noticed that Sister Superior had stopped saying much about the fort except when asked a direct question. She listened patiently to forty-one versions of what we ought to do about the College. But she kept her own ideas for the chapel where she spent hours in prayer, and it soon became evident that faith at the top exercised transforming effects all along the line. Whenever we failed to find her in the office, we looked next in the chapel and seeing her there in the deep quiet of the sanctuary, we understod how she could maintain serenity in the midst of so many uncertainties.

Sisters would come back from their appointments at the neighborhood medical-dental clinic and speak of the convenience in a manner reminiscent of pre-automobile days. Or they'd return from a shopping trip to town and enlarge on the absolute bliss of being able to catch a bus just two blocks away—every twenty-five minutes, too! They would sit down to a late lunch in our pink-walled dining room and sigh, "Isn't it wonderful to have everything we need right at our elbow?"

I knew that some of them were comparing conditions here with the fort. Two or three had been at Holy Names College the year it opened in its present quarters, and to them it must have seemed wonderful indeed. It really was when you remembered the early days at Holy Names Academy. I had been close enough to comprehend that.

On completing my canonical year as a novice, I had been sent to Holy Names Academy and Normal School in Spokane to continue my studies. "Mission novices" were those sent from the novitiate training center to one of the convents or academies in Oregon and Washington. There they had four months to get acquainted with the kind of life they might expect to lead once they had completed the period of preparation. The word "mission" gave the experience an apostolic and hauntingly foreign flavor, and I was ready, so I thought in my youthful zeal, for almost anything including head hunters and a diet of seaweed and sour milk.

Instead, I dragged my suitcase past the high cedar hedge to a massive red brick building, a monument to the days when French-Canadian bursars could still be talked into thinking that proper ventilation required 14- to 16-foot ceilings. The architecture must have been Dutch, taken over by Americans some time in the colonial period, and there were a lot of extra bricks that had little to do with shelter. The topmost of these had been painted orange-red, openly at war with the original brick.

Inside, the halls were long and narrow and stale-smelling; the stairways dark and steep, closed in by metal fire doors; and the furnishings clumsily ornate or severely simple.

St. Mary's Academy, Portland, Oregon, where I had attended high school, had been a remote preparation for Holy Names Academy, Spokane. Both buildings shared the same prisonlike atmosphere dating from a period when boarding schools walled off delicate young girls against the encroaching wilderness or the wild insurgence of a frontier town. At the Spokane Academy, there were the same multiplied passageways and stairs, the same dungeonlike compartments in an unfinished basement, the barnlike expanses of dormitory high on the fourth floor. But the halls were narrower, the stairs sagged more with the tread of ages, and the only cheerful spaces in the vast building were the chapel and some of the classrooms.

The Normal School students were insulated from the lower classes in one remote wing of the Academy, whither I used to find my way each morning for classes with the lay students. One of them was an apple-cheeked country girl who played an impressive cello and drove a car as expertly as if she had grown up behind the wheel. I soon acquired another job to supplement my study—that of helping the dean to type a new catalog, which we needed as we sought accreditation as a four-year college.

It was a good way to get oriented to the whole Normal School picture. In the weeks that followed, I had a close-up view between my classes and personal observation and my sessions with the dean. These last lengthened preceptibly as we neared the deadline she had set for taking the catalog in manuscript to a state Department of Education official. In Olympia the Sisters were cordially received by a gentleman who asked to keep the papers they'd brought, and we at home began the long after-hours task of making stencils of each catalog page.

Officials insisted that quarters separate from the Academy would be an absolute necessity, and the Sisters took a deep breath and said of course they'd have them.

Back home they thought of the half dozen Sisters who taught both Academy and Normal School classes, and when they looked out the window at their closely settled neighborhood, there was only one obvious place for the new college—across the street.

So they went over during evening recreation and buried a medal or two under the dust and weeds, remembered the poverty of their foundress, Mother Marie Rose, and reminded St. Joseph that, as protector and provider, he would have to do something about their need.

Four years later, when it was still recent enough to seem new, I had a chance to see what had come of the two Sisters' assurance: "Yes, we'll have a new building when we start this liberal arts program." On the acres where baked earth had made it difficult to penetrate the surface, their pledges of faith had sprouted miraculously. Over the shallow excavation their hands had dug now rose a simple two-story brick building. Set far back from the street, it gained in dignity from the expanse of green lawn leading to the front door, and at the left, it was joined by an arcade to a smaller unit, identified by its high ceiling and glass brick insets as a gymnasium.

In the front yard, a few dispirited saplings gave little promise of the birch, the chestnut and the pin oak they would one day become, and the row of maples in the front parking seemed unsure whether to die or grow.

I went through the arcade and into the side door of the administration building, feeling like a sleepwalker who had just discovered a solid object in the world of her dream. The hall was long, light, and clean-looking, as if the building were aware of its tenants' pride and reflected their joy in waxed floors and gleaming woodwork.

The superior showed me everything: the bare, bright

offices for administrators, with cupboards closed on Murphy beds and tiny washstands; the small, neat classrooms; the compact use throughout of stairway landings. Into this mezzanine were fitted rest rooms, a bookstore appropriately called The Niche, and the dean of women's office, outfitted with a daybed. Some of the music practice rooms were also equipped with daybed or daveno, for the Sisters had anticipated recent space-utilization trends and the notion of double shifts.

In the gymnasium, wells under the bleachers served as storage space for auditorium chairs. Backstage four music practice rooms doubled at curtain time for dressing rooms, and when I think of the nightmare of trying to teach in those rooms in the weeks of play rehearsals, I wonder how the Sisters ever managed when their bedrooms occupied the same space. They must have stayed up until all hours or else have gone to bed in a clutter of stage cosmetics to the rhythm of orchestra rehearsals, bouncing basketballs or amateur theatricals.

Still it was considered a privilege to sleep anywhere on the premises. The unit was primarily a classroom and administration building, and the faculty were content to wait nine years for a more satisfactory place to live.

Their real life was the classroom, and they warmed to it with the same spirit as the first twelve Sisters who came to Portland, Oregon, in 1859 and took their meals from planks stretched across two barrels.

The Sisters who were young and strong lived at Holy Names Academy and came over to the College building by day. I must have looked into the press room—backstage and upstairs—where my predecessor was even then teaching by day and sleeping by night, trying not to get the two mixed. But at that time I had no thought of ever being a college teacher. I was just headed for a year of study and had been told that I was to transfer to high school teaching when it was over.

The community room and chapel adjoined—two small rooms—and the Sisters' dining room was at the foot of a narrow, dark stairway leading to the library stacks. We used to joke that there was so little space that one had to step outside the door to change her mind, but the Sisters were so delighted with their independence from the Academy that such inconveniences seemed trifling.

By degrees the College achieved a more complete separation from the Academy. Its faculty no longer was expected to teach part time in the high school, and with the addition of a convent wing, the College Sisters moved out of their old-fashioned quarters into their happy mortgaged home. Just about then, the first advance notices about Fort Wright's being declared surplus must have appeared in Spokane newspapers, but at that time nobody even suspected that could have anything to do with Holy Names College.

I arrived the next year from the University of Oregon, duly heralded in the public press as the new Dean of Journalism at HNC. I discovered that I was not only the dean. I was the whole department! I had ideas, naturally, and proceeded to carry them out. The president was careful to keep me reminded that the institution had survived for more than a decade before I came, but the librarian bought the books I considered necessary, and the academic dean convinced students that their whole lives would be different once they enrolled for my classes.

And now we were contemplating a return flight to the primitive. Was there really anything to gain by the move? We had built a new residence hall for one hundred women five years earlier, and we had sold Durocher Hall, the old three-story home at Mission and Hamilton, in order to buy two small houses and lots across from the administration building. Wouldn't it be more prudent to give the grass a chance to grow under our feet? We had reclaimed most of the desolate acres between us and the railroad tracks. Another two or three years would bring the entire plot under cultivation.

After all the College was only twenty. What twenty-year-old doesn't make mistakes? We could claim our share, but we had known our successes, too, and it was people like Sister Clotilde who had been around long enough to tabulate them.

Sister Clotilde's intelligence and thoroughness were legend. In her early days at the College it was commonly believed that she would come through with flying colors at the state university where she studied for the doctorate. Nevertheless, she had the scholar's humble attitude toward learning and the nun's due regard for the formalities. Accordingly, when she asked for her Sisters' prayers on the morning she was to take her orals, a murmur of sympathy went round with repeated assurances of support:

"I gave you an intention at Mass this morning."

"I'll say my rosary for you.'

"What time are the orals? I'll pray in the chapel while they're going on."

As the refectorian joined the group, the examinee asked, "Will you say a prayer for me? I'm taking my orals today."

"I will not!" The speaker was a large Sister, and every pound was behind the emphatic reply. Then, as all eyes turned in her direction, "I'm praying for the committee."

There are times when it might seem the better part of prudence to pray for the committee, for the faith that can move mountains sometimes accomplishes singular results, and a Sister who has put the best effort of which she is humanly capable into her studies does confidently expect to receive a matching grant from the head office. Still, she is not beyond using whatever natural resources come to hand, even if these backfire occasionally.

One Sister, preparing to take her language proficiency examination in Spanish, consulted a predecessor for suggestions.

Told that her examiner always used a book from the library, she resolved to check out any books that seemed too difficult. The Spanish collection was small enough to make the precaution feasible, and Sister signed out two small books—one by an obscure Spanish poet and the other a philosophic treatise. Then she went home to review grammar and vocabulary.

"Good morning, Sister," the professor called out from the inner office. "I'll be ready in a minute. Have a chair."

Emerging a few minutes later, he cast a distracted eye about the room, motioned Sister to a place beside the desk and said easily, "I think I must have forgotten to bring a book. But I'm sure you have something in your briefcase."

Sister Clotilde herself had started the first school for the mentally retarded in Spokane. Her interest and professional training in special education had kindled enthusiasm among the college students and parents of children who needed special schooling. In time the venture was taken over by the local public school district, but not before Sister had demonstrated the dedication and energy such a project required.

In the preparation of other teachers, she had also made her mark. Public school supervisors welcomed cadets under her direction.

In art and music, the College had made many contributions to Spokane. Each year it sponsored the Northwest Circuit Show from the Seattle Art Museum, as well as other exhibitions in days before the city had a first-rate museum that would attract major shows. The music department brought such big-name artists and teachers as Guy Maier, Roger Wagner and Bela Nagy.

The Spokane Philharmonic had performed an original orchestral suite written by one of the Sisters, and it had been well received despite an amusing observation from the gallery.

"If that's modern music," one conservative listener murmured to her companion, unaware that a Sister two rows ahead could hear, "I'll stick to the classics."

Shortly afterward, the nun-composer was summoned on stage to take a bow.

"Clap for her anyway," the lady critic urged. "She has a sweet face."

A few years later I was able to write a story on two sizable science grants made to the College—one from the National Science Foundation, the other from the Atomic Energy Commission. The NSF grant was one of two made to colleges in the state of Washington that year for biology, and the amount of the Holy Names grant exceeded that given to the University of Washington.

These grants and the special equipment purchased with the AEC funds helped the department head to continue her special post-doctoral research projects and conduct experiments in applying nuclear technology to the life sciences. In-service institutes in science and mathematics drew students from all parts of the Inland Empire for Saturday sessions and evening classes. To help prepare elementary school teachers of modern mathematics, the originator of one method was brought from the Midwest to conduct special workshops.

The social science department sponsored a series of conferences on alcoholism. When visitors wanted to know what in the world a Catholic women's college meant by "getting mixed up in that sort of thing," the Sister in charge patiently explained that it was a human problem. Nuns ought to be concerned about every human problem, she pursued, and so successful was her involvement that she had soon won a spot on the executive board of the Spokane Citizens' Committee on Alcoholism. Many of the faculty attended the conferences and gained a good deal of insight into a problem that had been remote from their experience and their thinking. Among those taking the course for credit were a Salvation Army captain and his wife.

Our local newspapers were not staffed to cover the conferences, so I did both advance and follow-up stories on the entire series, phoning my releases in before I crossed the street to the faculty house to retire an hour or two after the regular time.

I learned a lot about human psychology during those conferences. I met some wonderful men and women, members of Alcoholics Anonymous, whose history was written ineffaceably on their persons, and I read in unmistakable characters the record of man's need for God and for human solidarity.

Language instruction in elementary grades was coming to the fore. Sister Maria had quietly organized a program of French classes for children at Holy Names Academy, starting with two grades and gradually carrying forward until all eight grades were included. The classes provided a laboratory for her College French majors working toward education degrees. She hoped that some day they might also net a few college students who would have a superior background for higher language study. She scheduled a summer institute for teachers, and soon Spokane's public and private schools had more language instruction by more competent teachers.

College faculty members were represented in 50 professional organizations, and they performed such services as testing, guidance, lecturing, and judging various competitions related to their special fields.

On the student side of the ledger there were other credits: more than 800 graduates had become teachers in public and private schools. Medical technologists and dietitians went on to successful internships. Social workers, journalists, secretaries, research assistants went out with their Holy Names College diplomas into a world where it was an accepted fact that more and more women worked.

Some, like Sister Edward, joined the congregation and later the College faculty. But most of them married and reared families. In that respect they were like the 93 per cent of American women who choose not to remain single.

The loyalty of our alumnae also encouraged us in our work. They came back to show off their husbands and children and tell us how grateful they were for their years at Holy Names College. They had gained more than technical proficiency and an accumulation of facts. They had learned a view of life, a sense of community, belief in the personal dignity and responsibility of women in society. We could hardly ask for more.

Joan took a position teaching home economics in a public high school. Her first pay check came back to us with a request that some other student have the scholarship opportunity she had received at Holy Names.

Little by little, our graduates became interested in studying for higher degrees. Lorna, a student body president who had worked in the library all during college, looked for a library school and applied for the most generous scholarship the state university offered. She got it and took her master's degree the following year. Dorothy and Jean and Leonore, biology majors, accepted research assistantships and went on for graduate study. Carolyn taught for several years, then enrolled in a university School of Journalism.

Many of our students dropped out after a year or two. But now more of them were coming back after their marriage to complete their studies.

The really brave ones started as freshmen anywhere from one year to twenty after they had said, "I do."

Marlene, who had married right after high school, decided that both she and her husband needed college degrees for the security of their family life. They moved from their small Idaho town into a Spokane duplex with her widowed mother-in-law. Ron enrolled at Gonzaga and Marlene at Holy Names. His mother took care of the four little stairsteps, all of preschool age. The fifth one came just in time to keep Mother from her semester exams, but she made them up and was graduated in the usual four-year period, even though she was taking a program that included a year's internship at a local hospital. Ron had attended summer sessions, too, and had begun teaching the semester before Marlene received her degree.

Frances waited until the children were old enough to help her do something besides practice patience. Her husband, a construction worker, was employed seasonally. Son Jim advanced most of his summer earnings for her tuition, and daughter Molly helped with cooking and housework. Both of them and the younger son, Pat, criticized the compositions she wrote for my English class, and the four of us finally got her through. She was one of the happiest and most attractive graduates in her class, and her teacher's salary will help Jim through his professional studies and the younger son and daughter through college.

It seemed to me that two or three success stories like

these made the whole effort worthwhile. Since research studies show that only one-fourth of all the young women capable of doing college work ever are graduated, we might be helping a few who would stop short of the degree except for us.

Some of the students who came to us had never before been in a Catholic school. Their parents sent them largely because they wanted their daughters to have the opportunity of living in a truly Catholic environment where they would acquire a rational basis for their faith and some sense of their heritage. Often it was a genuine awakening for the student, heretofore outnumbered, to come into surroundings where the things she believed were accepted by all her companions. She learned something about the wonderful power of the life of prayer, and she saw in the dedicated women who were her teachers an ideal of service that meant much to her.

Two or three abortive experiences had demonstrated the need for continuity in educational policy. We had started and stopped a one-year terminal course in practical nursing. We had introduced a course in medical secretaryship and allowed it to die quietly two or three years later. We had initiated a cultural series and built up a following through several years of steady promotion, only to have to let it lapse after it had attracted a following.

If we let Holy Names College die there would be no one around for a subsequent resurrection. It would be many times as hard to regain our current status once we had given up.

We needed Holy Names College. We thought that

Washington needed it too. Aside from the obvious service it performed in the undergraduate education and certification of our own junior Sisters, it provided the only program in the state where parents or their daughters who believed in the education of women *as* women, could realize that conviction.

It invited comparison and provided healthful competition for our other college at Marylhurst and our third Pacific Coast college in Oakland, California.

It necessitated higher degrees beyond the master's for numbers of our Sisters and so helped to raise the intellectual tone of the entire congregation.

It created the proper environment for the exercise of creative faculties in art, music, literature.

It engendered respect for the professional qualities of the Sisters and thus extended their opportunities for good into groups otherwise inaccessible.

It released leadership potential and talents that might be lost or wasted in a more competitive milieu.

It elevated the level of Christian culture in areas with few educational advantages.

But most of all it could give to young women a consciousness of what it is to be alive today. It could open to them the dimensions of the apostolate, make them know the needs of the world to which they belong. It could inspire them to exercise the intelligent interest, the compassionate eye, and the willing hand they had experienced in their own needs. For as Sister Emil, a leader in the Sister-Formation movement, has pointed out, it is a paradox that any apostolic job is done better by people who aim primarily not at the job, but at God.

Teaching is a spiritual work of mercy. And teaching teachers may be the same work multiplied. It means answering a need by compassion and help, as Christ would. So directly or indirectly, this established the goal for every Sister of the Holy Names College faculty, again in Sister Emil's words: "This is where our teaching apostolate fits in the religious life. This is what it means to teach as an act of mercy. This is the blueprint for a life which makes staggering demands of us, but which is unifying and which can be deepened from day to day. This means that we know the needs of the youngsters we deal with, that we train ourselves to see that their ignorance, their uncertainty, their problems, are truly miseries which call to us for direction, for confidence, for loving answers. This means that we look at the miseries long enough, steadily enough, generously enough, for them to move us to a great yearning pity and a burning desire to help."[1]

But in stressing the obligations of love it is possible to forget those of strict justice, to fall into the error of thinking that to do a good act badly for a high motive is praiseworthy. Here again, Sister Emil indicates with philosophic clarity the governing principles. Religious who accept students for professional services and take tuition from them or their parents enter into a contractual relationship. This binds them to perfect themselves as far as necessary in the subject matter they teach, to discharge their duties diligently and well, to do what they can to form the characters of their students and to give good example.

---

[1] Sister Mary Emil, I.H.M., "The Apostolate of Teaching," *Proceedings of the 1957 Sisters' Institute of Spirituality,* edited by Joseph C. Haley, C.S.C. Notre Dame, Indiana: University of Notre Dame Press, 1958.

The harm occasioned by an incompetent physician or nurse may be more evident and more dramatic than the intellectual damage wrought by an incompetent teacher. But the second is as much worse than the first as spiritual goods are superior to the merely material. All of this points up the dimensions of the teaching Sister's role.

She cannot afford to grow discouraged, for a failure to see the far-reaching results of her sacrifice may be the price God asks for her success.

His own teaching mission must have appeared unsuccessful to men of His time: in the apostolic college, one out-and-out failure, Judas; from the lips of the man Christ chose to lead His Church, denial; in the hours of His Agony when He relied on three to watch with Him, insensibility; and the reward of His three years' patient teaching of His chosen twelve, desertion by all except John. In the light of this record, it would seem that limited and partial success might justify years of dedication.

And then you remember Rosemary. And Catherine. And Monica. Confident, poised, intelligent, in their college caps and gowns—so unlike the frightened freshmen who came to the College, refugees from small high schools where anybody who did the assignments was an honor student. You want more than a piece of ground and a collection of buildings. Your real dream is a dream of realized potential for young women whose lives will be richer because of Holy Names College and a world that will be a better place because they have been there.

You know that you could operate more efficiently with double the numbers you now have. You could even accommodate that many and still not lose the personal contact that is one of your principal strengths. But what you want is something human and something good: it is no mere longing for prestige or power or material resources, though all of these things may help to achieve your goal. You have caught a vision of intellectual and spiritual wealth, and it is this vision you would kindle in those for whom it burns feebly or not at all.

You are not operating a Sunday School, and you will not substitute a facile pietism for genuine learning. But neither are you managers of a degree mill, and you cannot feign indifference when the progress of the mind bears no visible relation to human conduct. Although your primary responsibility is for intellectual development, you must try by word and even more by example, to prove that this is not enough. You are old-fashioned enough to believe that the most effective education adds to the sum of human happiness instead of producing a collection of misfits who are a burden to society.

You remember the great women who dreamed this dream before you and who dedicated their lives to making it come true, and you know that you cannot betray their trust so long as a wisp of hope remains.

CHAPTER VII

It was just about as unrealistic to expect the Sisters to agree on moving to Fort Wright as to expect a single opinion on a dozen other subjects including: our dress, liberal arts versus professional training, matrimony, Kennedy versus Nixon.

Sometimes I thought that we disagreed on everything except dogma. And even there, it would probably have to come straight from the Holy Father, citing chapter and verse of the officially approved translation with a special gloss to illuminate the text.

To illustrate, the Holy Father had said several things about religious garb. He said it should be simple, modest and expressive of inward dedication. He suggested that changes might be made to favor economy of time and the needs of hygiene.

Some of the Sisters were delighted to discover that, in our particular case, that meant no change whatever was necessary. They could wash and iron a habit in three or four hours, make one in three or four days, and when they looked around at a mass meeting of religious women, they were convinced that *our* congregation dressed simply.

Other Sisters rejoiced to know that *now* at last we might be delivered from the inhuman servitude associated with trying to keep mended, neat and clean in these primitive garments.

Those who envisioned immediate and drastic changes may have been disappointed to find that the first consultation succeeded in shortening the dress by one inch and removing seventeen inches of serge from a skirt that measured five yards around. Five years later another seventeen inches were subtracted from skirt *widths* and a lighter material authorized. This is hardly the place to take sides on matters of dress, but the controversy illustrates the differences of opinion that may prevail within convent walls on comparatively superficial matters.

At this point in time, it's difficult to consider my own religious habit with the detachment it might awaken in a stranger, but I do remember the curiosity with which I viewed it when I first went to high school to Holy Names Sisters. Much later, when I had been wearing the habit for many years, a lady who heard me speak in Yakima wrote to my superior to complain about my "blinders." Most observers are troubled by doubts about our lateral vision, but I suspect that it is far more adequate in the classroom than the inexperienced student realizes. But just ask someone who has been with our Sisters for eight or ten years. It's something like one-way glass: it's easier for us to see out than for somebody else to see in. And I understand only too well, from my journalistic activities, that we are the absolute despair of photographers whose whole training discourages having the subject look at the camera, but who must prefer that to a Sister without a face.

The next time I feel disposed to anathematize some fashionable lady's Easter chapeau, I promise to remember my first impression of certain religious costumes. Custom may not stale the infinite variety, but it certainly cushions the shock once the face underneath the awning becomes that of a *person* with definite traits and potentialities. Confronted daily with members of her own religious community, and introduced from time to time to those of other orders, the average nun takes the medieval dress for granted until she undergoes the traumatic experience of having fifty or more nuns, in town for a convention, break *en masse* and in mixed attire across the simplicity of her morning devotions in the parish church. Then she begins to comprehend the layman's problem and the exhortations to plainer dress that radiate regularly from certain clerical circles.

Anyone who assumes that nuns are "types" or that their views are duplicated in wholesale lots like those "patent insides" that used to be in some small country weeklies would have found a disorienting series of shocks at Holy Names College. We had, it is true, learned to predict one another's reactions as accurately as if we pulled the strings that governed the responses. But predictability and uniformity are not the same thing. Nor can we rule out the inconsistencies we early learn to expect of women.

When it came to matters more essential than dress—questions of educational philosophy, for instance—we might reach a minimum agreement. Everyone would hold, I believe, that it is the function of the Catholic college to educate students on two levels, natural and supernatural. But when it came to the relative stress each was to receive and the means to be employed in the process, ideas might differ sharply.

On the question of liberal arts and professional training, similar divergences of opinion exist. Someone might favor liberal arts in theory and be willing to relinquish essentials in matters of expediency. Or another might define liberal arts in such a way that the term fit neatly into the sequence mapped out for her majors and ignored some of the basics. Somebody else, taking what she considered a realistic view, might discount the liberal or subordinate it to the professional, justifying such a position by the need most students felt to prepare for careers, or by the demands of parents who were job-oriented.

Most of the Sisters would have agreed, I think, that education, to be complete, must train body, mind and character, none of which can be developed independently of one another. But whether that meant that every student had to suffer through prescribed physical education courses or that students must be penalized for class cuts was another matter.

Sisters disagreed on the independence that should be allowed to students. I felt that we were often inclined to demand too much perfection of detail without giving students scope. Our concern for the impression made by publications that circulated; our awareness that our College products might be unfavorably compared to others, sometimes induced an oversolicitous attitude on the part of the faculty. We were afraid to let students learn by making mistakes. We forgot that responsibility can be inculcated only in conjunction with authority.

Some of us felt that the students needed to be stimulated to disagree. Surely the world into which we sent them would not stand by approvingly and say, "Yes, dear" to every idea they advanced. If they became too critical in matters intellectual, of course, they might step over into faculty preserves and train their mental guns on some rather obvious targets. But that was part of the risk of running a college, and we couldn't refuse to take it because we considered nuns beyond criticism.

When Catholic educators speak of a unified philosophy integrating and directing the curriculum of the college, they refer more to a central view of man and his relationships than to specific courses or methods. This "center" provides the sort of freedom within law that distinguishes the best education from a search without a goal.

The farther we went from that center, the less agreement there seemed to be. The time to be spent in extracurricular activities and the relative merits of various kinds of them were a perennial topic for debate.

Our most serious rival for students was the state of matrimony, and the Sisters could be quite vocal on that subject too. We had a custom of inviting brides to return to the College and place their wedding bouquets on the altar. The Sisters sang a hymn, and the couple walked out to an organ march and signed the bride book in the small reception room. Then all the Sisters had a chance to congratulate the bridegroom and kiss the bride and ask questions about where they'd live. A few weeks later, somebody usually managed to see that the Sisters had a chance to look at the wedding pictures, left on the community room table until everyone had had a word to say about the newest alliance.

I often felt that we had a great deal of unused potential at Holy Names College. Not that the Sisters were lazy or uninterested or even complacent in any significant sense. But we needed something big enough to lift us out of the humdrum and quicken our faculties: something that would transcend the petty day-to-day routine and unite us in a magnificent endeavor in which all our powers could be caught up and concentrated. The raw materials were already there—the powder and the fuse, if you will—and all it needed was somebody to come along and touch a match to the thing, setting off a charge that would reverberate for a long, long time.

I was beginning to think that Fort Wright might be the match. I didn't know how we ever expected unanimity on that score. If ours had been another type of college, it wouldn't have been so necessary. The policy-making body would simply decide what was to be done, and the faculty could take it or leave it. If they didn't approve of the change, they could simply go somewhere else.

But Sisters are *appointed* to their positions each year by the provincial council, and if they didn't want to go to Fort Wright, they could just go there anyway. Or if they thought we should go to the fort and the council decided we'd stay at Boone Avenue and Superior Street, they could stay and make the best of it. This was what they bargained for when they took their vows of obedience, but until the directives of obedience were made clear, there was nothing to keep them from free discussion.

It was something like the situation in American politics. The presidential candidates and their followers battled it out in good-natured fashion, but once the party had selected its man and the campaign was on, everybody pulled together.

The Kennedy-Nixon debates were soon to have their echoes within the College halls, as faculty members took sides on a question where snap judgments often saw only one side. Many of the Sisters were staunch Nixon supporters, and those who weren't naturally began to worry about the preservation of the faith.

The Sister in charge of the linen room was an audibly enthusiastic Kennedy fan. She set up a suitably spontaneous "shrine" on the counter of her domain, and whenever we came in to iron we were regaled with the latest news items on the private and public life of the hero or treated to a glimpse of the Kennediana she had collected. The nominee's picture rested confidingly against a perfectly horrible statue of the Blessed Mother, walled in with towels or handkerchiefs or freshly ironed collars that had just come back from the laundry.

These touches of campaign domesticity were extended into the narrow dishwashing room that adjoined our refectory. A newspaper picture in color appeared over the sink one day as an appropriate reminder of the high thoughts we might entertain during these humble chores. Almost immediately, a larger, more brightly colored picture of Nixon took its place alongside. By lunch time Nixon had been deposed and Kennedy grinned down in solitary triumph. At suppertime the wall was bare again. It soon became clear, through some sort of unspoken communication, that the dining room and environs were under management distinct from the linen room. In other words, This Area Closed to Campaign Posters.

The linen keeper reined in her zeal and began to concentrate on the chapel for her major campaign, and evening recreation in common for "good works" to supplement her prayer. She would bring to each gathering some item of information about the Kennedy record, some testimonial from an unimpeachable source, some challenging item from a platform she had studied splinter by splinter.

We entered into the fun with lively spirit. When Kennedy was elected one of the Sisters forged a letter of commendation from his campaign manager and sent the Sister linen keeper a scrapbook for recording the new era in American history. She was undeceived and delighted, for she really did think that somebody should keep track of this extraordinary man and the miracles he was sure to set in motion. Meanwhile, some of the Nixon fans were threatening to chop down the next convocation speaker who pegged his talk to New Frontiers.

Even the lay faculty were amazed to learn that there had been a Nixon faction at Holy Names College. But then the problem of communication between lay and religious faculty in the Catholic college can sometimes be acute. I tried, for a while, to bridge the gap with a weekly news letter, later taken over by the president's office when she was relieved of her duties as superior. In our College, laymen were still in the minority on the faculty—a situation which we expected to continue for some time—but we realized the importance of their contribution and wanted to make them something more than second-class citizens. Fort Wright might give us help on that problem too.

One by one the members of the provincial council came to Spokane to see the fort property and buildings. In the bleak December landscape, "our" eighty-five acres looked more forbidding than ever. Winter had thrown a pall over the natural beauties of the site, and snow had not yet come to glorify the setting.

Mother Provincial and her assistant were shown into the battered buildings on one of the year's darkest and coldest days. Floors were buckling faster now, and plaster continued to fall. If somebody didn't move in here soon, there would be nothing left but ruins.

The contrast must have been painful, going from the clean functional College building not yet paid for into the cavernous cobwebbed darkness. The visitors returned to the College, and all of us watched their faces for signs. They passed the test.

"It has marvellous possibilities," Mother Provincial said. The Movers looked at the Stay-Put-ers and tried not to appear smug. Mother's assistant commented on the friendly sergeant, and the tension eased almost at once.

Not long afterward, the provincial bursar made the same trip. She had a different way of viewing things. When she looked at old buildings she saw repair bills. When she walked past furnaces she saw oil pouring in and estimated at once its rate of flow. And when she looked at a wall with that keen appraising vision, no overlay of romance could keep it from falling in. When she came back from the fort, the Stay-Put-ers looked at the Movers and this time the signals went the other way.

After that, it was open season all over again. With both sides licensed, arguments flocked from rival camps, to be picked off by the opposition almost as soon as they broke from cover.

It soon became apparent to all that certain Sisters had a genius for framing objections. Their talent was employed constructively in filling one column of the long lists of "For" and "Against," to be presented to the board of regents and to higher superiors.

Some of the Sisters were sure that the common purpose involved in moving and setting up a new campus would put new life and spirit into a faint-hearted faculty. Others were sure that the effort would be so taxing as virtually to incapacitate everyone.

Some thought that being farther from city center would lend distinction. Others insisted it would be *ex*tinction.

"Distance would lend enchantment socially," said the Movers. "Our girls are sure to have more dates, and the new site will provide greater diversity of recreational advantages."

"Distance will be an insuperable barrier," said the Stay-Put-ers. "College boys can't count on cars, and our girls will have to live dull lives in that No Man's Land."

The role of devil's advocate may seem an inglorious one. But a really efficient spokesman can do a great deal to consolidate the neutral and undecided forces, as ours undoubtedly did. To the incontrovertible evidence of a dwindling bank balance, the dreamers opposed the breathtaking intangibles of prayer and trust. Questions clarified goals and problems. Objections strengthened the will to forge ahead, in somewhat the same spirit that motivated St. Therese of Lisieux, who pointed out that, because of her very weakness and inconstancy, God chose to manifest His power through her, so that all might know the work for His, not hers.

The Jesuits from Gonzaga continued to inquire politely whether we were going to the fort. But I noticed that they had stopped smiling when they asked the question. And the sergeant who had showed us through the fort buildings had written a letter asking to stay on and superintend our physical plant at the fort when he was released from service.

Sister Superior was still being careful not to interfere with free discussion. Hers was the far-ranging eye, and I felt quite sure she was on the side of the Movers, but in a way wholly without anxiety or attachment. She simply put our whole future into Provident Hands and said, "Here I am for whatever You want. Use me."

Naturally, some of the more impulsive faculty members favored greater despatch in making great decisions. They complained that progress had come to a dead halt because nobody knew how to Get Things Done.

It was true that Sister Superior was not a whirlwind of efficiency. But you can replace an efficiency expert with a computer if you have enough money. Yet, confronted with the choice between a machine, even an impeccably shiny, clever machine, and somebody like her, who would hesitate to declare in favor of the one that turned out less work?

No matter how much we might like to rush things through we'd probably have to be patient. That was the trouble, I thought. We were always too much in a hurry, and I walked down the halls turning over a snatch of T. S. Eliot: "Teach us to care and not to care/Teach us to sit still."

Sister Maria had abruptly canceled her imaginary excursions to the American ruins and had turned her attention to academic matters with that almost stubborn firmness that was the secret of her accomplishments. She had arranged for two of her students to spend their junior year abroad. She was using standard tests to gauge the performance of her classes. And she encouraged language majors to apply for Fulbright scholarships and similar awards to pull up their performance level and give them broader goals.

Her own experience at the University of Montreal and later at the Sorbonne had taught her how much more most of us can do if the more is demanded, not just hinted at. And the results of applying that knowledge were soon evident in the quality of language instruction.

I wasn't really worried about what Sister Maria would do when and if we moved to the fort. Confronted with the inevitable, she would make public moan for a few weeks, working twice as hard during the process, and no doubt win a decoration for heroism beyond the call of duty.

Sister Philip had begun making ceramic lamp bases, mosaic tables and other articles of furniture that would be out of place in our present quarters, and one of the other Sisters was checking through a list of foundations for possible donors of building materials.

I watched all these signs of awakening life and wondered where they'd lead. And I felt just a little bit sorry for the Sisters who could not share in the spirit of adventure and the challenge of new beginnings.

I remembered the fourth-grade boy who had turned in a slogan for our centennial contest in the Oregon province: "Hurrah for the Holy Names Sisters, fighting all down the line!"

We could fight all right. It seemed to me that this was the project to unite the province. It would help all our Sisters to transcend local limitations and contribute to a pioneer effort unmatched since the days we joined in a crusade to maintain our schools, threatened with closure by the Oregon School Bill. We had carried that contest to the Supreme Court, and we had won because even beyond that, there was a Higher Law. And it was on our side.

Since we had only two colleges in the Oregon province, there was a good deal of faculty exchange, and I sometimes thought that we should send all the critics of Holy Names College to Spokane for a year and speed the solution of one public relations problem.

Sister Clotilde, with characteristic decisiveness, had made up her mind.

"If we don't put everything we have into getting Fort Wright and making Holy Names College the best in the Northwest, we may as well fold up and knit bed socks for the infirmary," she declared. Her look was so intense that silence fell momentarily on the community room where we were talking.

"Vinegar, Sister, vinegar!" one of the braver Sisters cautioned. "You've got a point there, Sister Clotilde, but don't drown it in vinegar."

"Why," Sister Edward interposed, picking up the bantering tone but with a quiet assurance that grew out of her long friendship with Sister Clotilde, "I think knitting bed socks might be a marvellous way to spend our time—provided, of course, we can learn in the meantime how to sit still and concentrate hard enough to count. Knit two, purl two, knit two. . . ."

By that time, Sister Clotilde was smiling herself. But not to capitulate too easily and disappoint her auditors, she fulminated a few minutes longer and sputtered to a stop, lips locked against the mirth that lit her eyes.

I wondered whether, with feet like Sister Clotilde's, I'd be so eager to join the infantry and march on Fort Wright. One route to the fort passed through *two* cemeteries, a way that seemed to me grimly symbolic of the crumbling bones on which our deliverance might be built. If Fort Wright were the answer, it would be costly, I knew, not in dollars only, but in human effort, buried personal ambitions and ultimately in lives.

But it was much better to spend our lives generously in advancing God's work for souls than to give way to paralyzing fears and finical inaction.

"Wisdom is more active than all active things," Scripture declares. Yet it sometimes looks as if evil and ignorance were far busier in our contemporary civilization. I could not believe that that was the way God wanted it.

Nor that He would counsel a timid reserve when the times called for heroism.

If the spirit of discovery in the sense in which Columbus must have known it has all but disappeared from our modern world, the blame is yours and mine, because the human hunger for greatness remains. Lacking a proper object on which to fasten, it turns aside as in the days of the Israelites to false gods made in the image of man's greed and violence.

But let a Dr. Tom Dooley come along, one man with courage, resourcefulness and the initiative to do something instead of moaning that nothing can be done, and thousands of young people are fired with the determination to help make this a better world.

I wanted to take part in something like that, and I believed that I could do it right where I was, in the very work I was assigned, for education is one of the most powerful of all agencies for good. I must not be satisfied with imparting mere information, though that was a beginning. Properly pursued, education should develop understanding—what Newman called enlargement—that breadth of view and awareness of interrelations that would make life worth living and man truly human.

Others had different tasks and different talents with which to accomplish them. Mine was to share the values I prized with those who were willing to consider them. We have been so dominated by exact science, so overwhelmed by the vastness of the Space Age, so conditioned to abjure our personal responsibility in the comforting presence of the experts, that we forget how much this country owes to those who regard their talents and aspirations as a sacred trust, for which they are answerable to God and to society.

As a nurse, I'd stand a poor chance of lasting a week, but in the classroom, I could go on and on, making with my students that mutual voyage of discovery that learning implies. Together we would watch the lonely seeker on his dark journey to a new world; the fearless questioner pushing into realms of thought his fellows had passed by; the stubborn visionary flying an improbable kite to wrest a secret from the heavens; the penniless inventor charging a filament with the weight of universal learning. Loving a country that was built on men like these, we might shake off our lethargy and dedicate ourselves anew to communicating our vision of the truth.

I remembered Dr. Albert Schweitzer and Father James Keller and others like them who have tried to prove to us what just one person can do, but the message takes time to permeate a mass culture, and I might be able to help speed it along in one little corner. I realized, with concern, that the cautionary voices had penetrated even to the cloister where a comfortable and orthodox mediocrity tries to replace the heroism of saint and martyr. But here, too, there were signs of renascence, and renewal of the apostolic spirit was in the air.

Once we had expressed an interest in Fort Wright we heard the timid voices everywhere: "It would take millions to turn Fort Wright into a college campus." "You'd need armies to maintain the place." "How many years will it take to establish a new identity and build a large enough student body to make it worth while?"

We didn't have the millions, but we thought we knew where to find the armies and the years. God's work would go on, and it was ridiculous to suppose that manpower and time could interfere with what He wanted. Maybe the very thing needed was a really difficult challenge that would unite the faculty in one tremendous common effort and tax their powers to the limit. After all, the blood of martyrs is the seed of Christians.

The fact that the College hadn't yet gone bankrupt gave the minimal assurance we needed to continue the struggle. When we looked back over a century of educational work in the Pacific Northwest we could see that all of the major advances had been made by women who were not afraid to attempt something difficult.

We prayed for light to know what to do, and for more than a year we hadn't had to do anything. The fort disposal was being cleared through the various branches of the service, then through other federal agencies. We held off on any further building projects, though we needed additional dormitory space.

Not quite two years after Sister Superior had clipped her story, the Lutheran School Board wrote to the City Council, making a formal request for fifty acres of the fort property. By the following November, our community room bulletin board suddenly carried a new and exciting notice: We were to indicate in detail the expansion needs

for our respective departments. Formal application was
being submitted for sixty to eighty acres at Fort George
Wright.

CHAPTER VIII

While three-fourths of the faculty were still trying to make up their minds whether the Fort Wright move was a good thing or not, Sister Edward and Sister Phillip had decided to act.

They reminded Sister Superior that it was only after burying medals in the vacant lot across from the Academy that the College property had come into their possession. It was not superstition, really, but just one of those devotional oddities nuns sometimes pick up in the course of living on faith. Nobody really believed, for instance, that turning St. Joseph's statue face to the wall would force him to intercede with God in the petitioner's behalf. Or that writing out a request and placing it on the altar during Mass would insure a favorable response from on high. All of these actions are merely external expressions of faith —indications that the person who does them recognizes the efficacy of the Mass as liturgical prayer, the intercessory power of the saints, or the relationship implied in honoring them. To insist on regarding these activities as primitive and literal would be equivalent to saying that Americans think the dead come up from their graves to enjoy the flowers and wreaths we lay on their tombs.

If the campaign for and against Fort Wright was to be carried on by prayer and sacrifice, everybody wanted to be in on the tactical maneuvers. Each Sister pledged herself to the program grace suggested to her. Though I suspected that we were not all praying on the same side, I had absolute trust in God's power and willingness to arbitrate the differences. Of course a Sister would be reluctant to move when she had spent years supervising the landscaping of the College grounds, bringing plot after plot under cultivation, working with yard men, storing bulbs each winter, setting them out again each spring. And how could a Sister, no longer young, who had spent some of the best years of her life working for the College, be expected to advocate the move when she knew that it would mean exiling herself from a place she loved? The distances between buildings at the new site, and the hardships of the pioneer phase called for younger, stronger, more flexible personnel. But I knew that, when the time arrived, all of the Sisters would come around and that whatever success the project enjoyed would be traceable in part to the sacrifice of those who favored the *status quo*.

Superiors might make a mistake so far as the standards of human prudence could ascertain, but that need not concern us. We made no mistake in obeying. Besides, no error was irremediable, since God could draw good even from human blunders; could even, as the Portuguese proverb has it, "write straight with crooked lines."

From the days of St. Peter, authority has played an important part in the organization of the Roman Catholic Church, and, as a natural corollary, in religious life. Yet the concept of authority is widely misunderstood outside the Church. It does not preclude the exercise of human reason as some maintain in an oversimplified view of obedience. Lines of authority in the Church are clearly defined, and directives actually protect Catholics from the misuse of power. Similar precautions exist to safeguard members of religious communities from encroachments, and part of the training of every Sister is thorough instruction in the nature of the obedience she will vow, so that she may make her public promise freely, knowing what and why she gives. She realizes that her submission is to God Himself through His visible representatives, who may, even so, represent Him poorly, judged by human standards. Surely there must be a few workers somewhere who do not consider their employers paragons of efficiency. Yet if they want to keep their jobs they learn to regulate their criticism, to keep silence unless the claims of justice or charity forbid silence. Is it surprising, then, that nuns should be asked to do something like that for a supernatural motive?

The sanction of authority, in the form of permission from Sister Superior, hastened the "prospecting" Sister Edward had planned. She had already chosen a spot to bury the medals after the time-honored custom of nuns everywhere, in the hope that this simple act of devotion might somehow reserve the land for apostolic work.

Blessed medals are known to Catholics as sacramentals, objects set aside by the Church to inspire good thoughts and animate the piety of the faithful. Their value as reminders depends on the dispositions (chiefly faith and the state of grace) of the subjects. They are intended to lead from the visible to the invisible, to act as stimulants or incentives. Their effects depend wholly on God's mercy, the official prayers of the Church and the dispositions of the user.

The Church has special formulas for the blessing of almost any object intended for human use, and though the ritual of the planting is strictly an extra-liturgical custom, most of us thought it no more superstitious than sealing odds and ends in cornerstones. It was a way of acknowledging confidence in God's power to effect the transfer of land if He wanted us to have it. As Robert Frost might say, "It was a kind of praying, I suspect. . . ." Hadn't Columbus' first act on reaching the New World been to plant the cross? And if the medal might be misunderstood by the military, Sister Edward explained, prudence suggested that it go underground.

It was a cold morning in late November when she got around to carrying out her intention. She whispered an urgent message to Sister Phillip after breakfast, picked up the keys to The Jewel, stopped by the furnace room to select a light, sharp spade, and arrived at the fort before the early morning sun had thawed the frosty ground.

Sister Edward parked the car off the road behind one of the duplexes in Officers' Row and then took the shovel and headed for the worn patch of ground she had chosen earlier. It was on the other side of the building, at the edge of the parade ground, in what she considered strategic territory, for there had been a question of reserving this land for residential use, and Sister Edward felt that we needed a "buffer area."

Sister Phillip hurried after her, carrying a small envelope full of medals: a Sacred Heart medal, a medal of St. Joseph, and a small relic attached to a picture of Mother Marie Rose, foundress of the Sisters of the Holy Names of Jesus and Mary.

There were no witnesses to the scene except a few stiff-feathered sparrows shivering in the gaunt shelter of a pine, hoping perhaps to find extra rations in the overturned earth. The spade struck with a grating sound against re-sisting clay, then, with the combined force of two pairs of black-sleeved arms, chipped out a small cavity which Sister Edward pronounced too shallow. They rested a minute in the keen wind, and Sister Phillip stooped to pick up one of the clods they had displaced and crumble it between her fingers with the ceramic sculptor's interest in texture.

"Maybe there's a clay pit somewhere around here," she said hopefully. "Did you look at the color of those banks as we drove over the bridge?"

They resumed their grip on the spade handle, Sister Edward clutching the top, Sister Phillip taking a lower grasp. They raised the haft, brought it down vigorously, and this time the blade cut a clean hole in deeper, damper earth.

"Let me take over a minute," Sister Edward said, lifting a worn shoe and balancing her weight on the tool.

A few minutes later, they were on their knees beside the small hole. Sister Phillip placed the medals in, one at a time, arranging them as she might the bits of a mosaic while Sister Edward led an "Our Father" and "Hail, Mary," her breath hanging on the frozen air like incense while the birds chattered and the distant rumble of an Air Force truck answered their urgent invocations.

They smoothed the sod back in place like a votive offering and rose to brush the evidence from their skirts. Sister Edward had just picked up the spade when a truck slowed past, and the sergeant called out, "Yawl on yard detail today, Sister?" He might have thought that they were looking for botanical specimens. Whatever he thought, he showed no disposition to investigate. And the nuns, on their part, were confident that no one could seriously question their innocent transgression. "Forgive us our trespasses," they had prayed, not without an intoxicating sense of propriety. But they were certain He would.

They returned home to keep vigil and wait, comforted in some sort by the thought of those medals, working like leaven in the unhallowed ground. But not before Sister Phillip had promised, "St. Joseph, if you get this property for us, you won't have to stay underground long!"

CHAPTER IX

Choosing a campus from the one thousand-plus acres of the fort was a challenge to the thrifty shopper. In a larger way, it was like visiting the supermarket for a choice cut of meat: the size and shape of the steak were governed vaguely by the contours of the animal, but within those limits, there was room for creativity and even a certain shrewdness.

The Sisters worked mainly from maps, which rolled from the duplicating machines of the Fort Wright headquarters office with mechanical regularity. And for those who felt ill at ease with the great outdoors and the mysteries of geography, there were floor plans for a multitude of buildings.

Our evening recreations turned into architectural musical chairs in which everyone walked in circles while Sister Superior read that day's newspaper story on the fort property. When the reading stopped, you took out your last sketch. If the Lutherans' school for boys was superimposed on your chapel or your home economics building hemmed in by Air Force Reserves, you just took another map or a different colored pencil and started over.

It was a time for decisive action. The slow and the timorous were left to teach in the furnace room, for expansion was in the blood those days, and it was considered a lack of vision to be satisfied with any space not double the size of one's present department. If you wanted to carry vision into the realm of hallucination, you could get a big roll of blank paper and draw a completely new building for your discipline, since the whole College presumably would collapse without it.

At one of these blueprint tournaments, Sister Clotilde raised her pencil point and surveyed her work. She had just settled the music building at the farthest remove from the education department, and she was forced to admit that such placement had much to recommend it. Never again would operatic ambition trill through the middle of her lectures.

Across the table Sister Edward proceeded on a wholly different plan. It showed the music department as the hub of the campus universe, so that all might share in the aesthetic clusters of sound that bounced or rippled from its confines during rehearsals.

Nearby, the academic dean concentrated on keeping odors from the chemistry experiments within humane limits. The aim had become identified in her mind with situating that department on the top floor. For seven years her office had been directly over the ground-floor chemistry laboratory; and since students were encouraged to perform their experiments on an individual time plan, spring had become for her, not the intoxicating season of flowers, but the suffocating ambience of hydrogen sulfide. It seeped into the walls of her sunny office, hung in oppressive clouds above her typewriter, and rolled over the wreckage of her afternoon schedule. What made matters even more intolerable was the dean's certainty that the fan, installed expressly to mitigate these horrors, switched on for only the briefest interval after she herself descended to inquire about the penetrating unpleasantness.

On the dean's plan, the chemistry building looked like an isolation hospital, with the actual laboratories perched on the fifth level, leaving a clean swatch of air for Old Glory and high enough to avoid soiling the clarity of a sky made bluer by white marvels of cloud.

The dean was having trouble disposing of the lower floors until Sister Maria quietly extracted a piece of paper from her pocket and flattened it out on the table.

"How about this arrangement?" she asked.

The dean nodded enthusiastically after proposing a few minor alterations. She began sketching the layout and listing its advantages in the margin. The chemistry teacher might consider the plant extravagant, and it would be wise to secure an ally in the architect. An academic dean with a degree in English literature could hardly claim jurisdiction in either chemistry or architecture.

The Sisters were so intent on their work that they hardly noticed the chemistry teacher's arrival. She had been looking over their shoulders for several minutes before she said anything.

"If that's a chemistry building," she began amiably, "you've put it on the opposite side from where I want it."

Then before the dean could present her first argument, "In *that* location we'd be asphyxiated when the wind blows from the east. Have you ever taken a deep breath within range of that meat-packing plant?"

More authoritative help came from the provincial bursar, who told us that the contractor thought the large buildings too expensive to renovate. We decided not to press our claim for any of them. Instead we limited our request to the somewhat newer officers' homes and some warehouses we thought might be converted into art and science buildings. The form of the section we finally requested was reasonably proportioned, including as it did a part of the parade ground, extending on one side to the bluff overlooking the Spokane River, and following the road on the other side. But at one end, near the loop, an eight-acre rectangle jigsawed into the outline to serve the national guard for vehicle storage and maintenance.

Faculty and students agreed that a bigger campus would make Holy Names seem more like a college, and the old buildings would give an Ivy League atmosphere—like adopting a tradition instead of waiting for one to accumulate. The three-story brick buildings that had served as officers' quarters made up in character and dignity what they lacked in compactness and convenience.

Adjusting their sights to larger dimensions, sports enthusiasts envisioned scope for tennis, golf, horseback riding; photographers considered hundreds of new camera angles; scientists planned campus field trips; and artists and thespians thought of open-air classes on the tree-lined campus.

But before anything like that could happen, there was the federal government to reckon with. And that was a process wound round with quantities of red tape.

Sister Superior and her secretary became expert in

bandying federalese. Files of correspondence with General Services Administration and with the Department of Health, Education and Welfare fattened as weeks wore on. Final approval of our application hovered always just beyond the bend of tomorrow, and repeated efforts to get something definite brought repeated vague assurances that after dealing with this or that entanglement a speedy settlement was expected.

Filling in forms kept the College administrators occupied, and the rest of us were permitted to state the imperative needs of our particular departments to lend urgency to the general plea.

On one occasion, the secretary had been closeted for hours with a typewriter and a detailed enumeration of our plans for every building on the section of land we wanted. Consigning the completed papers to Sister Superior for a signature, she pushed them thankfully into the nearest mailbox and waited for the next batch.

Back came a letter indicating that the uses for Numbers 18 and 24 had not been specified. Sister Superior opened her cupboard and extracted the roll with a permanent impression of her grip. The secretary helped her spread out the map, locate the numbers and consult the key.

Number 18, pumphouse. Number 24, flagpole. They looked at each other and began to laugh.

"We might as well put the pumphouse down for storage," Sister Superior said. "You figure out what to do with the flagpole."

I tried to convince Sister Superior that she should have told them the pole would be used to display the papal flag. But with Washington we were afraid to offer even such an obvious joke.

And so typed on letterhead bond with an IBM electric, over the president's signature, it looked almost as serious as some of the documents coming from the other direction:

Number: 18 Former use: pumphouse.
            Projected use: storage
Number: 24 Former use: flagpole.
            Projected use: flag display

Washington would be happy to learn that we were saluting citizens, loyal to the Stars and Stripes!

By this time our application had had enough notice in the newspapers to stimulate questions. At first they weren't hard to answer. We could say simply that we had applied and hoped to receive some of the property. Alert salesmen cropped up from everywhere and came to see "the Sister who does the buying" about everything from gasoline and portable classrooms to fire insurance, dairy products and laundry pickup service.

Nine Spokane schools taught by Sisters of the Holy Names boasted a total of 170 nuns, and since the fort prospect was a family affair, all of them had to see the possible new location of our College. Motorists driving through the property began to notice Sisters all over the place, and they wanted to know what kind of troops these might be engaged in their complex maneuvers.

We got used to making the loop down Custer Drive, leading toward Officers' Row, and we hoped it wouldn't be our Last Stand. There was still subdued but determined opposition to the Big Move on the part of some faculty members, and after the medal-planting story had made the rounds, an extra vigil light burned with a weak but steady flame each day before Our Lady's altar. I concluded that St. Joseph must have a competitor, that somebody evidently contemplated division in the Holy Family.

Some of the restless energies generated by the delay could be worked off in debating whether to change the name of the College, and, if so, to what? The obvious choice for those with a penchant for puns was "The Wright College for Women." Since Mother Mary Flavia, nee Alicia Dunn, had been one of the outstanding educators in the Oregon province, several Sisters thought we should change the name to Dunfort College, until some fatalist pointed out that it sounded too much like "Done for."

Sister Clotilde insisted that the name had to be changed; that the change should be decisive in order to avoid all possibility of being confused with Holy Names Academy; and that we should call the College after anyone who would step forward with a major donation. Sister Edward, who also favored a new name but couldn't resist a chance to tease, reminded her that such a policy had come very near to labeling our newest dormitory after one Mr. Spooner.

The physical education department worked off and on for a month, trying to think of a completely new name with the same initials so that the athletic letters wouldn't be obsolete. And the treasurer rechecked the bank balance and the supply of letterhead stationery, business

127

forms and other personalized materials, and decided that "Holy Names College" was probably the best name we could find anywhere.

I liked all this talk about a new name because it gave me something to say in news stories, and it didn't cost anything. The editor of the campus newspaper conducted an opinion poll on the name change, and the local dailies picked up the cue. Very soon everyone was talking about the name and citing the usual full-blown phrases from Shakespeare.

One morning early in July while I was teaching a summer session class, I was interrupted for an important telephone call. A reporter had just received a message from one of our senators to the effect that our preliminary application had been approved. This was the signal for full-scale jubilation, followed closely by a renewal of questions, some easier to answer than others.

Television sent a man to interview Sister Superior in the president's office, and I climbed around over the cables and took pictures of him taking pictures of her. We had had a short briefing session before he came and tried to figure out something as definitely indefinite as the statements sometimes made after diplomatic conferences. The property would make possible a new era of expansion and development. Our present quarters probably could be used by Holy Names Academy. When we moved would depend on the condition of the buildings and the amount of paper work to be completed. We would have eighteen months to get established and might need all of that time.

"Is it true that you're going to set up a road block and

not let any Protestants pass through the fort?" a photographer friend teased one day when I dropped into the *Chronicle* editorial offices to leave some copy.

"That all depends on whether we can get the Sisters through boot camp before we take possession," I answered. "But we'll probably make a few exceptions for those who contribute to the building fund."

A reporter joined us and wanted to know if we'd like to hear his lead for the City Hall session which had just been held to coordinate applications for property.

"City desk turned it down," he confessed, "but it went like this: 'Sections of Fort George Wright have been allocated to a Catholic women's college and a Lutheran boys' school, separated by the tanks of the National Guard.'"

It usually fell to my lot to figure out something to say to inquiring newsmen, a task that required considerable ingenuity in circumstances where, more than ever, we learned to live by the day. "Be not solicitous for your life, what you shall eat; nor for your body what you shall put on," Christ had said in the Sermon on the Mount. In that spirit, we were asked to live on the thin edge of nothing, our whole future hanging on a decision off somewhere in the other Washington, where the matter inched its mysterious way through the mazes of officialdom. We were practically operating a college out of a suitcase, and we might not have any students left if our status did not soon become more definite.

Every two or three weeks, some reporter was certain to ask about Fort Wright, and there wasn't much use in explaining that we had begun a new novena for the deed, or that Sister Superior had asked our chaplain to offer Mass for all the soldiers buried in the fort cemetery. I told newsmen as much as I knew, but from their point of view, it must have looked ridiculous. We were going to move the entire College plant out to the fort *if* we received the legal title in time. We hoped to start building soon after arrival of the deed, *if* we could borrow some money. We had ideas, we had hopes, we had unofficial assurances. In other words, everything except the legal title, the necessary capital, and a date more definite than "as speedily as possible."

I promised to keep my journalist friends informed, but they called regularly anyway, and as weeks passed without anything to report, I was forced to re-examine our position. Under the good-natured grilling any experienced reporter knows how to conduct, I got an outside look at the whole business. Divorced from faith and poetry, it looked rather grim. We were gambling on the slim chance that a bureaucratic decision would favor our application. If it did, our work would barely be begun. And a negative decision would inevitably mean a setback, for it would demand re-educating the alumnae, faculty and friends we had converted to the idea of a new campus. It seemed to me, though, that anything was preferable to the present uncertainty, and that the public might respond to a dramatic move even if it looked like magnificent folly.

Meanwhile, we couldn't afford to lose any of our friends, for we'd need all the help we could get, and we looked around for projects that wouldn't involve waste of effort and resources when and if we moved.

Even before the regional association inspectors confirmed our need for more books we knew that our library was inadequate. We added as much as we could to the budget and began to look for new ways to increase our holdings. Our librarian bargained and bartered and saved to make every dollar do maximum service. She built files of periodicals by careful search and exchange, haunted secondhand bookstores, put in her bid for library duplicates, and digested huge stacks of catalogs and bibliographies. She never missed a chance to apply for foundation grants or merit awards, and some faculty members were able to help her by departmental acquisitions from similar sources.

As moderator for the Holy Names Colleagues, I decided to ask the members to work for the library. Books would be essential, whether or not we stayed in our present location. The ladies warmed to the project and worked hard enough on card parties and rummage sales to contribute $500 the first year and more the next.

The alcoholism conferences brought a $500 addition to library funds from a foundation established to aid alcohol studies. The German teacher received a similar amount for adding materials that would help in preparing language teachers for elementary grades.

But even while we were helping ourselves with one hand, we were creating new problems for the other. More books required more shelf space, and both our reading room and stacks were pushing out the walls. The librarian had to spend too much of her valuable time trying to predict the direction and flow of book traffic. When she guessed wrong, or when preholiday book returns jammed up at the intersections, she paid the penalty in hours of hard labor, rerouting volumes until the next library excursion shifted mobile minds to another arterial.

We learned from Washington that an interim permit soon to be in our hands would precede the legal title to the fort property, and this indicated an even longer delay in building or renovating. Our business advisers assured us that it would not be wise to incur major expense until we were legally in permanent possession of the land. But we were reasonably sure we could house some students at the fort in the fall.

Under these circumstances the answers we did not know were asked for on an average of several times an hour. A prospective student and her mother would drop in and the conversation would go embarrassingly like this:

"Will you be having any classes out at the fort this fall?"

"I don't know."

"How many students will be living out there?"

"I don't know."

"How will they get to classes in town if you don't have class out there?"

"I don't know."

"What will happen to your buildings here?"

"I'm not sure."

"Well, when does school start?"

"We *think* it will be two weeks from today."

"Well, when will you know what you're going to do?"

"Pretty soon we'll be doing it. Then we'll know."

The Director of Admissions watched developments like

a broker checking on the fluctuations of the stock market. She could choose between becoming a cliché expert (You are enrolling in a College with a Great Future) and becoming the most unworldly of the daughters of Mother Marie Rose (You will live in the Providence of God, Who suffers not even a sparrow to fall without His knowledge). But, eminently practical person that she was, she settled for personal letters, individually typed, and mimeographed handouts that changed with the weather and the final fireside edition of the Spokane *Daily Chronicle*, indicating the status of the fort property disposal.

Already we were talking about our present quarters as "the old campus" until some alert individual realized that "new" and "old" were not very precise terms when the fort had a longer history than the Boone Avenue campus. We substituted "west campus" for the fort site, and "east campus" for our present one, and we began to feel a microscopic affinity for the University of California with its many branches.

Whatever normal hesitation we might have felt about moving to the fort before it was ready for us was offset by the imminent arrival of an overflow crop of boarders at the Academy. The previous year, the high school, bursting at the seams and haunted by the fire inspectors, had had to endure major inconveniences, owing to the fire department's refusal to allow girls to sleep in the fourth-floor dormitory. The Chicago school fire panic had spread westward, and even the costly installation of special doors, enclosed stairways, and automatic sprinkling systems had not been enough.

For this reason, high school administrators were as interested in our mail as we were. They wanted to know each day whether we were nearer a solution. The official documents seemed not to be forthcoming, and inquiries disclosed that nobody really knew where the papers were. Somewhere near the bottom of the pile on somebody's desk, we felt sure, but you couldn't go in and offer to help open his mail. They had left one office; they had not been received by another. Pages dropped off the calendar like autumn leaves, and we were powerless to act.

As usual the answer came when we had almost despaired of getting one. On a morning in late August when Sister Superior was sorting through the many deceptively urgent appeals for presidential attention, her eye fell on a fat missive with the official Washington return address. She slit the envelope eagerly, skimmed the contents with growing intensity, and went to the chapel for a brief visit.

This was the interim possession agreement but it took the rest of us a while to understand why the arrival of that document had not been the signal for general rejoicing. In a short time it appeared in the community room for our perusal. Those who persisted through the heavy legal terminology and the fine print had an inkling of the hesitancy that must grip the reader who decided to accept so formidable an agreement.

Once we had signed, we should be legally responsible for the upkeep and maintenance of the land and the buildings allocated to us. The government might at any time send inspectors to see whether our stewardship was satisfactory. If not, it was free to terminate the agreement and repossess the property. Temporary possession was not to last beyond eighteen months, and by the end of that period we must be in full operation there. Any improvements we made on the physical plant in the meantime were subject to loss if the grant of property were withdrawn, and we could not claim compensation of any kind.

Is it any wonder that Sister Superior grew more thoughtful than usual and that the treasurer came to meals looking pale and hollow-eyed? Contractors and architects swarmed over the fort buildings thumping here and tapping there, looking at foundations with X-ray eyes, checking with city hall on water rights and sewage disposal and related matters.

Sister Clotilde looked taller and more upright than ever. Like one of those hotel lobby plants two weeks after a Vigoro treatment. She could quote much of the interim possession agreement verbatim, and she went everywhere repeating, "Possession is nine points of the law."

The footsteps of incoming resident students grew louder, their inquiries more pointed; and the entire faculty stood at attention waiting for the word of command.

It came after a conference with the provincial administration at Marylhurst. Came firmly like the Voice of God out of a pillar of cloud. We were signing the interim possession agreement. We would house forty-seven resident students in three buildings at the fort. There would be less than two weeks to get them ready, and in the measure of our generosity God would surely give us strength.

A few days later Sister Superior went to the fort to receive the keys from a regional coordinator of the Department of Health, Education and Welfare. She accepted her commission like the soldier she was, knowing the heavy responsibilities it entailed, not knowing clearly how she might manage to meet them. But as she took into her hands that bewildering assortment of keys, she must surely have remembered St. Peter, the Keeper of the Keys. And if the fort could not, by any poetic flight, be likened to the Kingdom of Heaven, the work that was to go on there in preparing citizens for time and eternity might be.

We were now free to move furniture into rooms being cleaned frantically in an effort to keep ahead of the Holy Names Transfer Company.

And the Sister keeper of the keys smiled, recalling the promise Christ had coupled with the trust: "Behold I am with you all days."

CHAPTER X

Sister Phillip tossed three more tin cans into the trunk of The Jewel and shifted a roll of coarse wire netting and some garden tools to make room for closing the lid.

St. Joseph seemed to be keeping his part of the bargain, and she intended to keep hers. She helped Sister Edward ease a bag of powdered cement into the back seat where a third helper waited. Then she took the two rectangular pieces of plate glass Sister Phillip handed her, and moved her skirts aside while she slammed the door.

"Did you remember to bring the sketches?" Sister Edward asked as Sister Phillip slid into the front seat, trowel in hand, trailing several yards of twine.

Sister Phillip's blue eyes studied the sketches she had made of an outdoor statue of St. Joseph. "Roughs," she called them, and that they were. She had covered both sides of a used envelope with rude pencillings, one hardly distinguishable from the other to the average eye. But she seemed to be seeing something altogether beyond them when she looked.

Sister Phillip had never made a concrete statue before, but that didn't bother her. Nor did she stop to reflect that, legally, the College would have no claim to the statue when it was finished.

The terms of the interim possession agreement stated

clearly that any improvements made on the site (unless they were movable) should become the property of the federal government in case the agreement were terminated. But Sister Phillip had Sister Superior's approval for this squatter sovereignty in concrete, and she intended to install the saint while others, Martha-like, busied themselves about preparing a place for resident students to live.

Long before noon the trio were up to their elbows in cement. Sister Phillip's shoes already looked like primitive sculptures, and her veil twisted into an opaque grey leash behind her. Lime seemed to be winning in the struggle with cement, and every few minutes she tried to protect her raw and bleeding hands with a pair of rubber or plastic gloves, only to discard them again as they interfered with the shaping hand of the sculptor.

One of the Sisters had set up a short-order counter in a nearby wheelbarrow and mixed cement to specifications with a muscular energy that made passing airmen glad she was not the drill sergeant. The work proceeded in direct sunlight, and the sun proceeded without favoritism.

Sister Edward dragged a hose nearer and directed a jet of water at the torso, where a large tomato-can island still showed red through the rapidly drying cement.

"Hi, Sister! Good-looking space man!" the sergeant greeted them, pulling up beside the curb. "The Sisters said to tell you lunch is ready over in Number 11. How does that sound?"

"If they'd like to send us some Cokes," Sister Edward suggested, "I think we could stop that long."

They returned in sunburned concentration to their concrete problems.

Inside the houses, far from those ivory towers college professors are traditionally supposed to inhabit, we were on duty in our "fatigues." We had replaced our serge habits with huge coverall aprons, had gone through the girls' locker room leftovers until we found tennis shoes in the neighborhood of our size, and had armed ourselves with razor blades for scraping paint-spattered windows.

There were jobs enough to take care of the national crisis in unemployment, and space enough to allow for variations in speed and method. Solitary souls could start somewhere in the corner of a dark furnace room with the spiders, or off in a huge attic closet. More gregarious workers might choose the staircase, certain that they would meet almost everybody at some time during the day. For the meticulous and the antiseptic, there were plenty of bathrooms to be scoured and polished, and those with sure footing and a mountaineering spirit would exercise both by working on the two surfaces of windows.

Chimney sweeps played a major role in the proceedings, and the librarian staked her claim to fireplaces in living rooms and bedroms. There was place for every degree of talent and every quota of energy: drawers to be washed and lined with fresh paper; cracks in the plaster to be patched by a ceramist; chips in the wall paint to be retouched by the careful matching of an artist's eye.

Outdoor spirits had plenty of scope, too, for the Air Force had retained only a skeleton crew on the base, and lawns were browned to a crisp. Grass and weeds thrust themselves up between the bricks of the sidewalk, challenging the yard detail to restore the line between nature and art. One Sister spent an entire day manicuring the sidewalk before the sergeant gave a brief, but effective, demonstration with a potent weed killer that saved blistered knees and aching back muscles.

Like the members of some vast and industrious ant colony, the Sisters swarmed in all directions, carrying loads twice their size, making minute dents on the mountain of work that rose up before them. Airmen on their day off came over to help. Earlier in the week, the sergeant had assigned a couple to pry off third-floor window screens and carry bed springs to upstairs rooms. In the process they had caught our enthusiasm and returned to render overtime service.

Sergeant Nichols meanwhile extended his command to take in Holy Names Squadron and doled out demerits with good-natured severity: one for absent-minded professors who jumped barricades and tracked weed killer on lawns; two for Sisters who clogged drains by pouring dirty water into basins.

Servicemen learned to distinguish the Sisters long before they were able to memorize their names. They devised their own ID's, calling one "The Major," another "The Supply Sergeant" and a third Sister, who brought instant chaos to any territory on which she dropped, "The Bombardier."

We managed to snag a few early arrivals among the resident students, and drafted them for the cleaning crew in somewhat the same way we'd enlisted the airmen. They liked being in the advance guard because they could pick out their own rooms before the crowd arrived, and have the satisfaction of being charter members of the Fort Wright College.

The duplexes were in much better condition than the large buildings we had seen earlier, and we chose those least in need of repair for our first housing project.

It was easy to see that men had chosen the colors. And men surfeited with Army drab and Air Force blues, at that. We wandered from shocking pink bathrooms to kelly green kitchens to canary yellow bedrooms, our heads filled with domestic devices for reducing the glare without repainting. The psychology instructor suggested that we could assign rooms on the basis of temperament or incipient neuroses: the paranoid or melancholic in pink quarters, the euphoric in dark blue or brown.

Fireplaces in upstairs bedrooms were more decorative than functional—except for hornets. The Sister chimney sweep discovered a nest or two while she followed her sooty way from one hearth to another. The girls were particularly taken with the luxury of having fireplaces in their bedrooms, no doubt envisioning midnight marshmallow roasts. But by October they were writing home to Mom and Dad suggesting a pneumatic drill for a Christmas present. The fireplaces had been sealed with cement to keep wind from whistling down the chimneys. For our part, we sympathized with the residents over their cold hearths, but secretly congratulated ourselves on having one more fire hazard eliminated.

Remnants of an ancient bell system connecting the back

hall with the servants' quarters on the third floor tickled our democratic funny bones. Practical Sisters joined with the imaginative in a chorus of admiration for the dining room's bulky old steam radiators, whose doors concealed a spacious bun warmer, where frostbitten college girls could toast their toes if the kitchen failed to appreciate supplementary ovens.

One detail of architecture seemed to make a duplex complex. There was no passageway from one half of the building to the other, and it was necessary to go out the front door, or the back, to get to the other side. This doesn't seem like a very big problem when it's a question of one family visiting another family. But when a dozen pajama-clad college girls want to see what's going on in the other half of the dorm, it may mean that the Sister housemother joins the porch patrol. Eventually, it seemed wiser to cut a doorway through the living room wall than to have a housemother divided against herself.

The next problem was furniture. Most of the Sisters didn't read *House Beautiful* or *Better Homes and Gardens*. But they knew all about how to turn some No. 10 tomato tins and five or six old boards into bookshelves. They could make a quarter go farther at the warehouses of Goodwill Industries and St. Vincent de Paul, where they found whatever they couldn't beg or borrow from the attics and basements of friends' homes.

Sister Edward made it a standing rule to show gratitude for every donation, no matter how ugly, and she had plenty of chances to apply the principle. When you tell grade school children to bring anything, they bring anything. In the middle of lunch Sister would be called away from table to accept from a nine-year-old's hand one cracked cup and a bent spoon.

"Our Sister said you needed dishes for the fort," a third-grader would explain, and we'd hear Sister's exclamations of delight and visualize a set of sterling silver. But it was just as Sister said, "Beggars can't be choosers," and for every worthless object we received, there were two or three that would do until it was possible to replace them with something more attractive, harmonious or convenient.

The girls who lived at the fort that first year raised no eyebrows over mix-and-match china or a Duncan Phyfe dining room chair beside an F. W. Woolworth magazine rack. We had bought two small houses and lots across from the College a few years earlier, and the owners had included some of the original furnishings. When one living room was turned into a language laboratory, and the other into a bedroom, furniture was stored in the basements, along with some extra mattresses and a few end tables. Those of us who lived in these faculty houses could follow the furnishing of the fort duplexes by remote control, simply by checking on what items had disappeared from our basement. But the furniture hunt was not limited to storerooms, and anyone who had more than one of any single item risked having it confiscated. The trick was to make everything look indispensable, and the tidier you were at housekeeping, the harder this was to do.

If a refrigerator had nothing in it, next day there was apt to be a smudged place on the kitchen wall where it had been disconnected and removed. If a chair seemed one too many to fit at the table where the others stood, it suddenly took on the power of self-motion like the tripods of Hephaestus, and a desk with empty drawers was regarded as an open confession of superfluity. Everyone understood that most of the furnishings would eventually be moved out to the fort campus, but in the meantime, it was a question of outfitting two campuses with the equipment of one. It's expecting a good deal to ask a college student to bring her chair and table service with her for every meal.

Everybody who wanted to help out could. A Sister with a weak heart devoted one whole day to de-squeaking doors. Another decided to feed the hungry and prepared daily lunch for the cleaning crew.

We postponed College registration another week and were able to open the duplex doors on that revised schedule. St. Joseph, solid if somewhat prematurely hardened, stood in place at the end of "The Key," and a large HOLY NAMES COLLEGE directional sign pointed clearly under the one reading AIR FORCE RESERVE HEADQUARTERS. We liked being able to put up as many signs as we pleased, for in Spokane authorization from the city council was required, and we'd had trouble getting permission to hang our shingle at the Boone and Hamilton intersection.

Our industry was beginning to pay returns: in our section, islands of green lawn rose up in a sea of brown. Sidewalks cut a tidy brick swath past houses whose windows gleamed in marked contrast to the opaque dust of the unused buildings; and wide front porches, hosed down after thorough sweeping, welcomed visitors into living rooms whose cleanliness looked less bare as it filled with September sun. The scent of fresh floor wax blew down the curved stair, its ivory balusters innocent of dust and fingerprints, and from farther back in the kitchen, the fragrance of fresh coffee and frying hamburgers signaled the lunch hour.

But people had to see in order to believe. Many Americans have an unglamorous mental picture of Army life, one which they are quite ready to extend to the Air Force, if not the Navy and the Marines. Uniform rows of ugly barracks, planted inconveniently in the middle of nowhere, disciplined without apparent regard to common sense or human values. Transfer the picture to a women's college, and you'll understand the opposition we encountered when we talked about moving to Fort Wright.

Mothers were not sure whether the quarters would be comfortable, and some of them seemed to harbor a lingering suspicion that the troops still occupied the territory and the poor Sisters didn't guess the trouble they wanted to move into. A few of them insisted on a personal inspection tour before they would consent to have their daughters live there. I suppose that if we had moved the entire College plant instead of one-third of our resident students, there might have been less cause for alarm.

We had one dormitory in town for upperclassmen whose health, schedule or attitude eliminated them as pioneers. But very soon after classes started, Boone Avenue boarders were wishing they could move out to the fort: it seemed as if everything exciting happened there.

The Candy Rogers Case had filled columns in the local

newspapers since the day the sunny nine-year-old had disappeared while selling Camp Fire mints. Police had traced her as far as the bridge leading to Fort Wright, and they speculated that she might have drowned or met with some other accident, though the possibility of violence was not excluded.

While the *Spokesman-Review* set up a woman reporter in a local hotel to receive the confidences of anyone who cared to give information about the case; while local clergymen appealed for the return of the child if she had been abducted; and while police continued to pick up and question suspects, the mystery remained unsolved.

There were literally thousands of hiding places in the fort's dark old buildings, cut off from daylight as from artificial light. It had tempered our enthusiasm for exploring our possible future home to think that we might be visiting the scene of tragedy or terror.

But we did not realize then how the horror would cling about the place; how in the imaginations of newspaper readers who had never been on the site, the suspicion would grow to certainty and the certainty to irrational fear.

Mothers were too much concerned over the safety of their daughters to reflect that the fort property covered more than one thousand acres, that it was relatively abandoned at the time of the child's disappearance, and that, when the child's body was finally found, it was on a remote wooded area, far from what might be our College campus. It would take time to erase the association with that crime, even though we knew perfectly well that the fort was as well protected as our town campus.

I made the mistake of arranging an innocent picture of two girls on the porch of one duplex. The overline said something about college students moving into former officers' homes. Not long after, a member of the Colleagues told me of the indignation among women who supposed that the girls were out there without any adults. I reflected somewhat bitterly that I should have written: "Not pictured are John Smith, Pat Brown and Don Green who live in a house (not pictured) on the fort site and carry shotguns. Also three Sisters who see to it that dormitory regulations are observed but are just too shy to appear in this photograph."

There were still a few die-hards on the faculty who thought we should give the fort back to the government. They would have returned Oregon to the Indians, Louisiana to the French and Alaska to packs of admirably adapted polar bears and seals.

And there were problems—chief among them, the fact that the deed had not yet arrived, and that we couldn't possibly go on for another year with two campuses.

Everybody kept saying that it was just a matter of time until the deed came through. First of all we were going to have it by Christmas. Then there were a couple of technicalities that should take until the first of January, and "very soon after that" we might expect it. Whenever an important feast day dawned on the liturgical calendar, some Sister was certain to decide that the deed would arrive. The fever spread, and chronic optimists would hover around the Superior's office at mail time like prophets looking for a sign.

I was sure that the deed would arrive an hour or two after one of our campus newspapers had gone to press. The deadline schedule of a monthly newspaper seldom permits breaking any really big news, and together, the staff and I decided that we would be ready. We set up a shot of the president conferring with the Sister in charge of fort development. We had a halftone engraving made and put it in a pressroom drawer ready for use. One of the reporters researched local newspaper files and turned out an historical feature story. We decided to have enough pictures of the West Campus to cover us in any important newsbreak.

As the person responsible for news releases and copy for brochures, I became expert in the art of the indefinite statement. Since our whole future was in doubt, and no one could predict the moment at which the yards of red tape woud finally unsnarl, I had to be careful not to date my copy by referring to buildings and physical facilities that might not be ours the day after the mailing piece rolled from the presses, or by making a definite statement regarding a building that might be reassigned several times before the prospective student set foot on the chimerical campus.

I'd sit down at the typewriter and turn out copy like this: A COLLEGE ON THE MOVE. (That was a sage beginning, since we live in a world of flux, and movement need not be physical.)

"Eighty-five acres of scenic campus at the heart of the historic Fort George Wright property have given Holy Names College room to grow." The number gave a precise ring to the sentence, and so far we were not committed to anything except "room to grow," and nobody could dispute that. "Colonial-style homes, former officers' quarters, house residents in compact, family-size living units." This came dangerously near saying something, but the truth it hinted at was fairly certain, as we already had two and one-half duplexes in use as dormitories, and we expected to convert others to that use as soon as we abandoned Marian Hall on our town campus.

"Others of the twenty brick buildings are adaptable to requirements of administration, art, music and library," the blurb continued. Not "will be adapted to" or even "have been allocated to," but merely "are adaptable." Adaptability seemed to be the major entry in the College lexicon.

The rest of the flyer dealt with things that were likely to be unaffected by federal decisions: "Ten minutes from city center, the campus overlooks the Spokane River, enjoys a view of the city and of Mt. Spokane, blends Ivy-League atmosphere with exciting new developments."

Sometimes I felt like annotating the text with such observations as: "Of course, nobody knows what these exciting new developments are. Not the College president, not the faculty, not the students, so by what claim do you feel entitled to an accounting?"

Instead, we accompanied the evasive text with a few sketches, which we assumed would satisfy the curiosity of prospective students regarding the quarters in which they might live and work. Since there was nothing even remotely resembling a classroom on our portion of the property, I added the line: "Classrooms, housed in new buildings, will provide for a growing student body." Where and when these new buildings should mushroom was a debated question, for prefab had not been considered, so far as I knew, and it was already too late to build a major structure in time for fall classes. But we covered our empty phrases with the standard closer: "For further information write Director of Admissions" and inscribed a fine map of the fort property on the reverse side of the mailing piece. The map showed the area of the fort for which we had applied, the section assigned to the Lutheran boys' school, the eight acres reserved by the Army National Guard and other solid certainties such as the main gate, the George Wright monument, the Downriver Golf Course, the edge of the bluff and streets like Northwest Boulevard and Government Way. Perhaps it was not the best promotional piece ever created, but it was something to put in an envelope when a student wrote to ask for informaion about Holy Names College.

Between times, I amused myself with parodies of my new style on this order: "You will be housed (or at least roofed over) in a house and/or houses (possibly tents) and go to class (if we ever get a schedule) in classrooms (*i.e.*, kitchens, parlors and other walled-in areas). The College is (in) conveniently located (*location* here bears the flexible Hollywood sense) on a site and/or sites northwest and/or east of city center with frequent bus service (though possibly not in your direction). The scenic campus (all campuses are scenic) covers 4.8 and/or 85 acres overlooking the Spokane River [*Both* our campuses overlooked the river, but the one in town sported the less-than-scenic waste from a cement plant along its borders] and commanding a view of Mt. Spokane (with 24-hour prospect of freight cars in foreground)."

I had to file that one with Publications That Never Got Published.

It had now been more than four years since we first looked forward to the fort move, and we sometimes seemed no nearer a settlement than at the beginning. Everyone was carrying a double load this year because we were maintaining two campuses with about the same personnel we'd had for one. The Sisters who were housemothers at the fort had the heaviest duties because they assumed these tasks in addition to their former full-time jobs. With a number of smaller living units at the fort we'd need even more Sisters for housemothers, but we knew that the girls would have closer contact with them, and they'd probably like it better, as they used to in the days before we built a larger residence hall.

The pioneering spirit is a good morale builder provided you don't overdo it. And high morale, as every psychologist knows, favors physical fitness. The Sister infirmarian noted with satisfaction that the Sisters were working harder than ever, yet nobody seemed to be ill.

But I knew that the present schedule couldn't hold indefinitely. Neither the students nor the Sisters could take it forever.

After five 12-hour days the girls needed a weekend break, so meals at the fort were arranged for them from Friday evening to Sunday noon. Each duplex had a kitchen with a hot plate for snacks, but only one had a full electric range (family size). That meant bringing huge pans of food on Friday evening from the College kitchen five miles away to feed more than forty hungry women. The Sister in charge went efficiently about her task of warming and serving supper, always hoping that the cooks would remember she had only one oven and three burners. An all-oven meal would have to be served in courses, and it already took long enough to feed the occupants of three homes in a kitchen and dining room meant for one.

By spring the fort girls were thoroughly converted to their new home and neighborhood, reluctant to leave even for classes in town. The air was cleaner, the sun brighter, and the atmosphere more peaceful in that suburban setting. They begged rides from the few residents with cars, coaxed the day-student drivers or their boy friends to taxi them home after classes, and spent all the time they could spare from the library in their country retreat.

But if they were won over to the new campus, day students and those resident on the town campus were not so sure. The freshmen came from their flawlessly furnished lounge at Marian Hall to visit the colonial-style homes at the fort. Ushered into the entry way, they removed their wraps and walked into the living room. Here they saw an austere combination of early American and late St. Vincent de Paul. Floors were of hardwood with wall-to-wall polish. In one duplex white woodwork offset chocolate brown walls, and several pieces of borrowed modern furniture, upholstered in white plastic, harmonized with the color scheme if not with the period. A small television set in a turquoise plastic cabinet flickered from a clumsy pine table. Beside it a lamp, stiff and graceless, diffused a pale, impenetrant light.

The fort fleet managed to get to classes every day, even when roads were icy, and St. Christopher took a hand in proceedings to keep our battle-scarred cars running. Sister Maria had won her driver's license along with her wings and you could often see her head for the jaunty little Jewel, a real diamond-in-the-rough, cavorting over snow-piled roads with the eagerness of an aging freshman. There was a brief interval when a huge loose-jointed bus rattled down Boone Avenue looking as old as Boone himself, and the sweet eager faces of college women looked from surprised bus windows over the three-inch letters BISHOP WHITE SEMINARY. After the bus came The Bullet, a spasmodic Pontiac whose engine died at intersections or shot suddenly through a red light when you'd just begun to miss the sound of a motor. Along with all of these ran a reliable Ford, a forty-niner and pure gold by College transportation standards. The sergeant brought a carful of collegians on the way to the school his two older children attended, and another ex-airman on our staff drove his car.

Meanwhile our architect was drawing plans for classrooms. Spring and the building season were coming toward us headon. Church-state agitators were collecting signatures protesting our entrenchment at the fort. Sister Superior and her secretary were writing to persons of influence, asking their intercession in securing a speedy settlement. And Washington answered all our entreaties with formally polite letters telling us what we already knew.

CHAPTER XI

One of the things we already knew was that night seems darkest just before light breaks.

But like so many other things, this truth had to be relearned as experience presented it under different circumstances. As nuns we had no particular immunity to suffering, and it is often an ingredient of spiritual trials not to be sure that they are trials. God works in the soul in hidden ways, and He does not want or need our self-conscious analyses of what is going on. Yet a life under the vows of poverty, chastity and obedience must be preeminently a life of love. The very nature of love is to go out of itself in order to give happiness to the beloved even at the cost of great personal sacrifice. The interlocking of joy and sorrow is basic to the human condition. An unadulterated diet of either would quite simply be heaven or hell.

There is a notion current in certain circles that Sisters live in a romantic utopia. They float from the chapel to the cloister garden on clouds of incense, secure in a haven to which the anguish and uncertainty of modern civilization seldom penetrate, and then only as a pleasant sort of contrast to make them realize how serene it is to inhabit an atmosphere above all that.

If there were not a grain of truth in this idea it might never have gotten started. An understandable reluctance to dramatize her suffering contributes to the impression that the nun doesn't have any.

"It's so peaceful here," the visitor remarks, and for the Sister who has not yet learned how to squeeze into the sixteen waking hours permitted by her Rule the responsibilities of eighteen, the peace may appear to have gone underground. It is only when she returns to the world most people live in that she realizes the difference between it and the convent.

In "The Tranquillizing Influence of Other Whales," a modern poet speaks of the false sense of security engendered by the crowded city with its many distractions, and concludes thus: "Protect us, crowd, with the blessing of commotion./No need to think now, in the human ocean,/ Nor to remember, much less fear,/Where the tranquillizing influence of other whales is so apparent."[1]

There should be no whales in convents. Daily in the solitude of mental prayer, Sisters confront the ultimate realities. They share in the universal agony that transcends time. They are Christ's chosen ones, and He trusts them with the burdens of a suffering world.

In a civilization where so many persons must be endlessly distracted; where we have forgotten how to call upon our own resources for entertainment; where joy and cheer are synthetic responses conditioned by a television screen, or merely the names for detergents, it is refreshing to find somebody who radiates happiness. "Joy is the echo

---

[1] Marian Storm, *Saturday Review*, December 7, 1957.

of God's life in us," someone has written, and if the expression is to be more than a slogan, one must see it actualized in the person of those who have consecrated their lives to God.

There is something terribly wrong about a cross, ill-tempered and unhappy nun. Nor does this mean that Sisters must be devoted to empty optimism or childish indifference to the evils and anxieties of our modern world. Unthinking repetition of the phrase, "Love is blind," has made us forget that the deepest love is remarkably clear-eyed. We cannot love God intensely and remain unaware of His suffering children in every land. We cannot ignore the tensions created by nuclear weapons or the very real possibility of having our world blown to bits through some individual's heedlessness, stupidity or malice.

But perfect love casts out fear, and it is in the measure of its trust that the soul's love registers as genuine. If we consistently meditate three important truths, let them penetrate our consciousness, try to live by them, peace in the deepest sense can be ours. These truths are: God knows all things. He can do all things. He loves me.

Convent life provides specific time periods for such reflection. It makes room for silence and solitude, for manual labor, for study and recreation. But secular life does not altogether eliminate the possibility of solitude, though it does make it more difficult to come by. It is partly a matter of the value we place on it, for one may have no genuine solitude even in the midst of isolation.

Isolation wounds, constricts and terrifies. Solitude heals,

enlarges and fortifies. Today there is very little left of this healing solitude and, in our crowded cities, far too much isolation.

But there are still a few persons left who recognize the need for a measure of quiet and for interludes of privacy. That is why it is possible in our society for parish organizations to make money by selling tickets to an evening at home; and why jukeboxes sometimes include among their selections two minutes of silence.

St. Catherine of Siena, placed among fatiguing distractions and given the most menial tasks by her relatives, withdrew into an "interior cloister" and found deep union with God. So often our agitation and our multiplicity are not external merely, but reflect the turbulence of our own disordered ambitions.

The intellectual life requires a degree of solititude, as anyone knows who sincerely undertakes to pursue it. This is why Sisters who go on to graduate work should have an initial advantage. More and more teaching Sisters are taking degrees at top-flight universities here and abroad. Gradually administrators, even in some of the secular institutions, are beginning to realize the contribution the Sisters can make. To attract them, they may even make special living arrangements better adapted to the Sisters' needs.

One large state university reserved a sorority house for nuns during summer session. The following year, with more Sisters enrolled, the director of housing turned over one floor of a large women's dormitory for the exclusive use of the nuns, but some of them wanted to have the same accommodations as the preceding summer. So there were two kinds of semicloistered students: the sorority Sisters and the dormitory Sisters!

The nun who leaves her convent for a secular university is like an astronaut who must be conditioned to live in outer space. She cannot afford to relinquish her prayer life. Separated from her Sisters, she will look for God in the lives and hearts of strangers, alert for every indication of their need. The Will of God becomes her cloister and the Providence of God her sanctuary.

Sometimes outsiders think this means that the life of the nun is a perpetual honeymoon on a more rarefied level. But the love of God, like human love, is the work of a lifetime, and it is often most real when it is least discernible to the senses. We are a combination of body and spirit; and it is this body-soul unity that must be joined with God in love. But anyone who supposes that this precludes sorrow and dryness and difficulty must be very naive indeed.

It is in this sense only that convent life can be called monotonous. It is monotonous in the same way that life or marriage is monotonous. But it is often erroneously confused with the monotony of a false heaven.

The reluctance of some laymen to warm to the idea of heaven indicates their misconception of it. If either paradise or the cloister conformed to such versions, reluctance would be understandable. Sometimes I call the inhabitants of both these pseudo-heavens "confectionery characters." They are popular in certain magazine fiction and in greeting cards "For a Sister in God's Service." But I confess that

I have no more sympathy with these sugar-coated shadows than with the plaster saints whose poeticized lives were the despair of my early strivings toward holiness.

I know now that God works in and through time; that He prefers to transform, rather than destroy, the human, lighting it from within in a way that makes goodness genuinely attractive, not artificial, unimaginative, or self-righteous. Holiness must make man more of a man or it is not holiness.

The average layman is attracted, not repelled, by the idea of dedication. His uncomprehending attitude toward Sisters, if he has one, is not concerned with the fundamentals like the life under vows, or obedience to certain rules and regulations, but rather with the externals, with matters of protocol like names and dress.

Reluctance to call a nun "Sister" or "Mother" according to the practice of the order sometimes places the layman of another faith in an awkward position. He may imagine that the term connotes some kind of endearment or intimacy, or, at the least, a tacit acceptance of Catholic tenets. In reality this is a courtesy title, no more fearful nor familiar than the word "Dear" in the salutation of a letter or "Miss" in the preface to an unmarried woman's name. Unlike the "Miss," however, it can be used with perfect propriety all by itself, a tip that should help many a reluctant layman to address nuns with polysyllabic names excavated from the Roman martyrology. "Sister" or "Mother" is meant to suggest the spiritual relationship which ought to exist between the nun and everyone else: that of loving concern for the genuine good of every person created in God's image.

While preparing a television panel with two other college representatives, I had occasion to make a number of telephone calls to a sectarian college. Whether I talked directly to my colleague or through an intermediary, I met with the same embarrassed perplexity. The person at the other end of the line would ask how it was proper to address me; I'd answer that it was just fine to call me Sister. We'd finish our conversation. Then I'd hold the receiver and wait for the voice to take a running jump . . . "Yes, I'll give that message to Mr. Downs when he comes in. And thank you for calling . . . that is. . . . Well, I'm very glad you called." About the third time, the caller usually managed the hurdle and said—right out loud—"Sister." After the first time it was easy.

As we sat under the glare of the television lights waiting for our cue, Mr. Downs mopped his brow and grinned in my direction.

"I bet it's hot with that thing on." He motioned in the direction of my headdress. "What do you call that thing?" he asked, indicating the white linen gauze that framed my face.

"It's a coif."

"Coif," he repeated after me. "Coif . . . coiffure! That's what's under it!"

If you happen to be one of those shy Presbyterians, take heart!

A few communities of religious women retain the use of the family name, but most of them change the name completely to symbolize the new life the Sister enters upon when she takes the veil. The name chosen, either by superiors or by the candidate herself, usually is that of a saint or angel, though it may link the name of a saint or some form of Mary with one of the mysteries of Christ's life: for example, Sister Mary of the Crucifix. When a large number of Sisters enroll at a university, there is likely to be duplication, and this renders use of the family name imperative. So you walk into a class with several Sisters and are treated to the oddity of hearing roll call: "Sister E. Duncan, Sister Annette Murphy, Sister Evangelista Quinn" and so on.

After one of these sessions at Notre Dame, which the Sisters found highly amusing, especially since the IBM machine often cut them off in oddly arbitrary lengths, one of the students went up to her professor after class.

"You can just call me Sister Elizabeth," she said amiably.

He gave her a startled look followed by a stiff smile.

"Thank you, thank you," he said with strained gentility. "And you can call me John."

Next to the problem of names, that of dress seems to cause the most comment, and if you want a layman's view you can probably get it in one easy lesson the next time you take a taxi.

The cab driver hunched over the wheel, a burly fellow, tossing an occasional comment or question out of the corner of his mouth and lowering one shoulder, as if to let the remark by on its way to the back seat, where I sat stiffly in the middle of all that space trying not to stare at the meter.

"Say, what do you people have—two outfits, one black and one white?"

"No, we just have one," I told him. "But the different

162

habits (That's what we call them) distinguish the different *orders* or *communities*." I felt like a foreign language teacher, carefully building up vocabulary to establish a medium for communication.

"There are more than three hundred *orders* in the United States alone," I continued, studying my pupil for signs of restlessness.

The shoulder dropped again. "Well, I saw two of them yesterday," he said, "and they were just completely, all snow-white."

I thought of their black veils and decided to skip them for the moment. "Those were *Dominicans*," I said, articulating the word slowly and carefully, but I could see that I had lost him.

"Well . . ." His tone indicated that this subject, like the weather, was quickly exhausted. "I hear that there's a bunch of them in New York that have gone over to reg'lar clothes."

"I think that those are Sisters of Social Service," I said, and by now I was ready to stop, too. He clicked off the meter, opened the door, and let me out of my Classmobile.

The next day as I stood in the lunch line looking like twins with another Sister of the Holy Names, I recalled my experience with the cab driver for her and one of our summer acquaintances. The girl laughed almost as appreciatively as Sister, and I was encouraged.

"It's the strangest thing," I commented. "Even when a whole group of different kinds of Sisters are together, lots of people don't notice that we dress differently."

"They just aren't very observant," the girl said with a tolerant smile. Then turning to me and my companion, in identical attire right down to the brass-bordered crucifix and rimless glasses: "Now I don't have any trouble at all seeing that you two are different."

At the time I thought that the public lacked perception, but I have since learned to look with a more understanding eye on the layman's perplexities. There *are* Sisters who have two outfits—one black and one white. There are communities that dress one way inside their convents and another when travelling. The problem is further complicated by the many congregations which have "modernized" their dress in recent years, in favor of a garb easier to make, mend and keep clean. The increase in the number of Sisters driving cars has also been a factor in modifying the headdress of some Sisters.

Some orders, with an impressive history and headdress to match, have become so familiar to Catholics and non-Catholics alike that to change their format would be like introducing a tabloid makeup into the pages of the *Kansas City Star*. Much depends, too, on the point of view of the observer: the portrait photographer, the poet, the artist may grow enthusiastic over a costume to which he would react quite differently if he did the weekly ironing, or sat beside the wearer on a crowded bus, or behind her at a concert.

More professional students of religious habits, like the men students at Notre Dame and Marquette, have a specific name for each order, and to the most alert listener goes the largest collection. Without distinction, or because

164

of it if you prefer, the Sisters' academic reputation has merited the title of DAR's, and I'd probably start another American Revolution if I substituted anything but a discreetly Victorian stroke for the adjective preceding Average Raisers.

The Daughters of Charity of St. Vincent de Paul are popularly known as God's Geese; the Sisters of the Holy Names as Dutch Cleanser Girls; Religious of the Sacred Heart of Mary as Parentheses or Gothic Arches; the Congregation of Notre Dame as Steeples; and the Incarnate Word Sisters, with their white habits, red scapulars and blue embroidered emblem, All American Girls.

Because certain groups are native to particular regions, their habit is familiar to Catholics in those areas who may never have seen nuns from another part of the country. Transplant a Sister from her usual habitat, and she is sure to be addressed by every third Catholic she meets, asking "Sister, what order are you?"

The fifth or sixth time around, the question gets monotonous, and you'll feel like saying, "Human order. And you?" But you don't. Instead, you smile sweetly because you know they expect it, recite the full name of your congregation, toss in its usual abbreviation for good measure, and enumerate the states in which the species may be found. You get so you know right away when you're outnumbered, and, with the woman's instinct for society, you gravitate toward the random individual who welcomes the sight of your habit with affection and esteem.

Members of certain orders, like the Benedictines, who branch out to establish independent foundations as soon as their numbers reach a certain level, create another problem for the uninformed. Although they retain the same name, the same basic Rule, and a similar dress, minor differences exist and are apparent to the astute observer.

At a midwestern women's college, an excited student from Boston rushed up to a Sister of St. Joseph and began asking questions about some of her former teachers. Sister had to confess that she didn't know any of them, that she belonged to a distinct group of Sisters of St. Joseph, "one of the twenty-seven varieties" as she put it, and that she herself was from Kansas.

"Oh," said the student, her eagerness deflated, "I always thought that Sisters of St. Joseph were something nobody had but Boston. Wait till I tell them when I go home."

So far from home, it's a pleasure to have anyone nod familiarly in your direction and say, "Holy Names Sister?" You feel as if you have been rediscovered.

What incentives do Sisters on a college faculty have for professional excellence? Obviously, they won't be discharged if they continue to use the same lecture notes for ten years without reading anything new in their field. They may, of course, be transferred if found unsuited to college teaching, or they may be given another assignment just because, in the overall plan, they are needed elsewhere. But what about excellence in their profession when they aren't working for promotion, except in holiness, and are not subject to the usual rewards of merit, such as tenure, a raise in pay or the chance to choose their own courses and class hours?

First of all, they have their religious Rule, which, in a

teaching community, provides for a double purpose: personal sanctification and the education of others, according to the directives of the constitutions of the congregation. By profession, then, they are religious and they are educators, and they are to become holy in and through the apostolate of teaching.

Secondly, there is the matter of motive or intention. If we are really working for God, as our whole way of life declares, can we afford to do a shoddy job? In most areas of human endeavor, the quality of the performance bears some relation to the dignity of the purpose for which it is done. If we say we are teaching college women for the glory of God, we had better look to the caliber of our teaching.

Thirdly, we have the papal directives, more insistent in recent years when renovation and adaptation of religious life have been the subject of careful deliberation. The Vicar of Christ has urged that the preparation of religious educators should equal or surpass that of their secular colleagues. With such encouragement in high places, Catholic educational leaders have been increasingly outspoken in self-criticism and with heartening results. The case is put very succinctly by a bishop who said, "Those who defend mediocrity in the natural order, even in the name of supernatural striving or supernatural achievements, neither speak nor act the mind of the Church."[1]

---

[1] The Most Rev. Joseph M. Marling, C.PP.S., S.T.D., auxiliary bishop of Kansas City, Mo., in *The Mind of the Church in the Formation of Sisters,* ed. by Sister Ritamary, CHM. New York: Fordham University, 1956. p. 20.

In the light of such considerations it becomes even more important for the college to keep *alive*, not just existing. It must be alive intellectually, morally and physically. And as the whole basis of private education in the United States shifts, the small college perhaps feels more than any other the problems created by rising costs and demands for expansion. Unless it is heavily endowed, as ours is not, there will be moral threats as well: invitations to despair or (worse still) to an ostrich-like complacence. There will be the temptation to court intellectual disaster by the effort to succeed at all costs, even quality. But if the college is really alive, it must combine the long view with a clear and serene awareness of the contemporary scene.

Sisters whose life work is education cannot afford to be less than outstanding in their profession, and this standard applies not only to elementary and secondary schools, but especially to their colleges.

Sisters believe that there is no law against *teaching* just because one is engaged in higher education. Critics have consistently maintained that some of the worst teaching that's done goes on at the college level. Of course one doesn't need to coddle students, but there seems to be no sound reason for making intellectual activity dull and uninspiring.

For in this educational league the Big Ten are commandments, and the first of these is the love of God, which is never really love unless it is reflected in the love of the neighbor. If there is any stronger motive for excellence, I don't know where you'll find it. Then isn't it time we stopped being afraid and flung ourselves in one magnificent gesture into God's work? Holy Names at Fort Wright thus becomes not just a narrow field for personal defense, but the symbol of every great and daring commitment of a woman in love beyond recall.

CHAPTER XII

Time magazine has a tidy little plan for keeping the Creator separate from His creation. It consists in putting anything about God in the classification labeled *Religion* and everything else in some other department. Once in a while it becomes unavoidably apparent that classifications overlap, and then the trick is to push the news item firmly under one of the headings and hope that nobody will notice.

But sometimes they do. A group of Sisters on a nation-wide concert tour, for example, refused coverage of their musical activity because editors insisted on classifying it under Religion. Now unless this insistence were a comment on ineptitude (something I doubt very much in view of the Sisters' skill), it does seem foolish to contend that when a layman plays Mozart, it's music and when a nun does it, it's religion. On the other hand, there's a sense in which the concert could be called religious for both, inasmuch as all creativity partakes in the divine creative action.

In the quest for truth, the goal of higher education, we cannot limit ourselves to truths of the natural order. Divinely revealed truth, the subject matter of theology, must have an integral part in any complete system of education. And because errors about God lead almost of necessity to errors regarding the nature of man, it is extremely important that theological instruction be competent.

Actually, *Time*'s procedure doesn't differ essentially from hundreds of similar practices of a secularized society. The world our students are going to live in tries to put God into a seal-tight compartment marked "Open only on Sundays and in case of emergency." Such a civilization isn't likely to provide a congenial climate for the theological habit of mind. For that reason, the college theology program must be doubly effective in order to give to society Catholic leaders who will be good thinking Catholics.

Unfortunately, this hasn't always been the case. About twenty-five years ago, theologians woke up to the fact that religious instruction in the Catholic college needed a shot of vitamins. In analyzing the split between Catholic higher education and apostolic zeal, they concluded that the trouble stemmed partly at least from the lack of solid academic grounding in theology. Courses failed to measure up to the standard set by those in other departments.

With the laity taking a more active role in the life of the Church, and with Sisters playing an increasingly important part in higher education, it was inevitable that the need should be felt for women trained in theology. To meet this need, St. Mary's College, Notre Dame, opened the first School of Sacred Theology for women in the United States in 1943 and merited papal approbation in 1949.

Some of the faculty were recruited from the Dominican Fathers who had embarked on a plan to restore theology to what they regarded as its rightful academic role. This now constitutes their largest single apostolic work in the

United States, where they teach theology in about seventy Catholic colleges and publish books and periodicals on the subject.

Traffic in ideas on theological instruction has thickened considerably in the last two decades, and, as usual, travellers have different ideas about the most efficient way of getting where all of us want to go.

As Father Robert Henle, S. J., pointed out in an interview with Donald McDonald, "There is a lot of room in Catholic education and in the Catholic philosophy of education for a variety of opinions. We have some fundamental principles, but these do not dictate down to the last iota how you are going to run a school system."[1]

Catholic educators agree that the ultimate purpose of education is identical with that of life itself. The primary responsibility of the school is for intellectual formation—for training in the arts and sciences. But this is a principle of order or subordination, not one of exclusion. Man's intellect and will cannot be divorced, and at every level, but particularly in the lower schools, moral education must be provided for.

Jesuit education with its traditional emphasis on the study of philosophy differs in many respects from the Dominican plan. Some Jesuits advocate a "humanistic" approach to the study of theology. Even though there are Dominicans who object to the opposition of that term to their own "scientific" designation, the labels do seem to point up a difference in stress.

---

[1] *Catholics in Conversation*, J. B. Lippincott Co., 1960. p. 258.

It looks like a healthful situation to have these two strong currents of educational thought flowing through some of the darker passageways of Catholic higher learning. For it seems to me that theology may have suffered even more than other disciplines from the false dichotomy between learning and holiness. Besides, this controversy can stimulate inquiry and help both sides to maintain balance.

While we were preparing for a revaluation by the Northwest Association of Secondary and Higher Schools, we had an opportunity to reconsider our goals. Inspectors were not likely to quarrel with them, we knew, but only with the relation of means to avowed ends. They were accustomed to deal with a wide variety of colleges and universities and they were like passenger agents on a train who never asked why you wanted to go to Blankville, but only whether your ticket would get you there.

I had read of one large secular university whose philosophy department made this tendency the basis for a "descriptive" approach to the target. Instead of setting up objectives, professors conducted a survey to discover what effect philosophy courses had on their students. Then they made what happened their aim.

We didn't want to join them in doing things backwards, but it was important for us to check our results, as well as our methods, against our goals. Like most Catholic colleges we professed to consider theology and philosophy the integrating forces in the curriculum, and we were beginning to realize that just publishing the statement in the College catalog didn't make it come true. When we say that theology integrates, we mean that as queen of the sciences it orders and directs the other human sciences. But at the same time, it recognizes and respects the mode proper to each.

Outsiders sometimes ask whether theology courses in the Catholic college are geared to making converts or to the lay apostolate. The primary object of college theology is the imparting of a science, of an intellectual habit. But theology is both speculative and practical because its single object, God, is both a Truth to be known and a Good to be loved. The successful theology course puts the student in a position to live and act wisely. It equips him for intellectual leadership, perhaps the most important apostolate of the Catholic college graduate.

This was what we wanted to do, and though we knew it would take a lot of experimentation and research to discover the best way in our special circumstances, the ideal was worth working for. And if we were successful, alumnae would continue to educate themselves in the highest of acquired wisdoms. One of the major goals of theology professors, as of other faculty members, ought to be that of convincing students that education is never finished this side of the grave.

I have occasionally been present in gatherings of alumnae that forced me to ask, "Where have we failed?" And I have gone back from them to the classroom, more than ever determined to plant deep in freshman minds the seeds of discontent with intellectual atrophy.

The content of theology is the whole body of revealed truth. Its sources are in Sacred Scripture, the writings of the Fathers and Doctors of the Church, the liturgy and customs, the decrees of Church Councils and papal pronouncements.

Its method is scientific in that it proceeds from principles (truths assented to by faith) to conclusions. It might be called human reasoning about divine truths. Some educators deny that it is a science insofar as its principles are accepted on faith and are not directly verifiable. But its premises are based on the highest kind of certitude: the authority of God Himself.

Emphasis in teaching theology will be partly determined by immediate goals and by contemporary conditions. For example, lay students will normally require more thorough study of the theology of marriage, and current problems may require added stress on such principles as that of racial justice.[1]

It is quite generally agreed that the college should provide an environment for participation in the liturgy, and to that end we hoped to have a student chapel at the fort. But classrooms would have priority for collegians, and Sisters might have to be content with a small oratory in the convent. If it were in the cloistered area, students would not have access to it.

Sister Maria was beginning to think that she might lose the one job she wanted most to keep. She reasoned that her ability to hold down a bigger job might disqualify her for

---

[1] For many of the ideas expressed in this chapter I have drawn rather freely on *Theology in the Catholic College*, ed. by Reginald Masterson, O. P. Dubuque, Iowa: The Priory Press, 1961. Whatever distortions have resulted from the attempt to translate them into popular language are my own.

sacristan of a small convent chapel. For the past year she had found that preparing for daily Mass and keeping vestments and altar linens spotless, work though it was, gave her genuine joy.

All of the Sisters were concerned about what the students would do without a chapel, but Sister Superior, who might have been expected to show most solicitude, waved objections aside and simply asked us to wait. It almost looked as if she had some particular assurance, and I, for one, felt sure that she had.

In the interval, she directed her attention to academic problems. A couple of years earlier, the Oregon province had begun a self-study to revaluate its entire educational program. Some of our most capable Sisters were directing the inquiry.

In examining the courses of study at various other women's colleges, we noted that St. Mary's had raised its requirements for undergraduates to fifteen hours of philosophy and sixteen of theology. Students had the option of offering the upper division courses as a minor. Non-Catholics must fulfill the philosophy requirement, but were excused from theology, since that study proceeds from principles accepted on faith.

The emphasis thus given to the study of theology seemed more consistent with the usual catalog declarations of belief in its importance. But adapting the principle to the local situation made me think of a magazine sales promotion letter that started: "By camel, by droshky, by metro, by jet. . . ."

Naturally, theology teachers would want to go by jet,

but with our small student body and limited faculty, we'd probably wind up doing a solo flight or crashing into antagonistic mountains. It might be better to settle for a less speedy but more suitable mode of conveyance. There was a lot to be said for an efficient camel, compared with an inexpertly handled jet. And by the time we had a larger assortment of licensed pilots and a longer passenger list, we could trade in some of our droshkies and camels for more high-powered vehicles.

Teachers of philosophy and theology, like those of mathematics and science, would need a retread to keep up with advances in their fields. And teachers in other departments would need a good foundation in theology and philosophy.

Sister Maria, I reflected, was a good example of the kind of faculty member needed outside the theology department, to effect an integration of the students' learning. The teacher was the bridge between theology and the other sciences and arts, and in order to succeed, it took somebody with her liberal background and comprehensive view. To proficiency in teaching modern languages she joined an active interest in learning of all kinds. In Europe she had taken advantage of every opportunity to learn more about philosophy and theology and she continued to read and investigate them on her own.

At the fort she had eyed with alarm the possibility of losing precious class minutes because of the distances between buildings. She had promptly borrowed a bicycle to avoid being tardy. When some of the Sisters raised eyebrows, she cited no less an authority than the late Holy

Father, Pope Pius XII, who had commented favorably on this practice. Then she peddled off to class—on time!

Sister Maria was as good an example as any of the harmony that could exist between scholarship and the religious life. The notion of an essential conflict between them seemed no more valid to me than that of a disparity between art and the religious life. Both research and creative endeavor depend on a contemplative atmosphere and have often flourished in monastery and cloister. And though most Catholics agree that in principle it may be better to feel compunction than be able to define it, in practice the statement has too often been used to pose a false choice between learning and holiness. Or to cloak academic incompetence in a mantle of false piety. If faculty members can command students' respect both as teachers and as religious, they will be better able to communicate that love of learning essential to education.

Sometimes the student does not really consolidate her gains until her values have been challenged. One of the most rewarding experiences available to the teacher in a Catholic college is to see the intellectual and spiritual awakening of a graduate who encounters for the first time a system of higher education put together without God. The confrontation suddenly makes all those years of Catholic education come alive in a wholly new way, as the student realizes what they were all about. She recognizes her roots in the rootlessness of others; her faith in their unbelief; her spiritual riches in their poverty. For the first time she understands what it really means to be thankful. She is no longer content to know her religion in some vague, ill-defined way, for she realizes that it must be vital or it is a mockery.

Nor should the recognition make her smug. It is part of the function of the Catholic college to give the student a rational basis for the faith that is in her. If there is too marked a discrepancy between sacred and secular knowledge, a Catholic is apt to undervalue his religion in much the same way that the concert pianist brought up on newspaper verse takes a dim view of poetry.

College helps to make the student articulate about her religious conviction. Not that she must go about proselytizing twenty-four hours a day. Her life will often be her most effective sermon. But she should be able to discuss doctrinal or moral issues with those who ask about them and to regulate her conduct according to her beliefs. With the recent stress on "dialogue," this interchange is even more important, for many of the old barriers have fallen, and we can no longer insulate ourselves religiously, any more than we can subscribe to the kind of nationalism that was current before the League of Nations. This is why the presence of the nun and the priest on secular campuses is even more important today than it once was.

I remember a young Jewish student at a state university who once said to me, "You and John sure do play hell with my stereotypes of nuns and priests."

"That's good for you!" I assured him, and we embarked on an exchange program quite unlike the National Conference of Christians and Jews, but, I am convinced, equally effective.

For my part, I am glad that I live in an era when

Catholics no longer pray for "the perfidious Jews," for "heretics" and "infidels," and have begun instead, during the Church Unity Octave, to ask forgiveness "For acts of violence and the injustices we have tolerated in the course of history against our Protestant brethren" and "For proud complacent attitudes shown . . . towards our Orthodox brethren, and for indifference to them."[1]

For everywhere today people who once considered it in poor taste to discuss religion now are doing so publicly and in print. And because many non-Catholics lack courage to address nuns and priests, the lay Catholic, and particularly the Catholic college graduate, has an even more important work to do.

He should do it patiently and with respect for the honest doubts of others. If his faith is more than an heirloom, he cannot be indifferent to its reception by those he respects and loves. Religious indifferentism is an open confession of religious sterility. Can you imagine a truly dedicated artist who is satisfied to have his friends' art education limited to *Saturday Evening Post* covers? Or an ardent believer in the art of fiction who is happy to find his students on an exclusive diet of confession magazines?

The Catholic believes that Christ established one true Church. It is logical, therefore, that he should burn with Christ's own ardent desire, expressed in that prayer to the heavenly Father: "That they all may be one, as thou Father in me, and I in thee, that they also may be one in us; that the world may believe that thou hast sent me." (John

---

[1] Litany for Church Unity prescribed by the Most Reverend Leo A. Pursley, Bishop of Fort Wayne.

XVII, 21) The "faith without which it is impossible to please God" is, as His Holiness, Pope Pius XII, has indicated, an entirely free submission of intellect and will. Yet the Catholic truly aware of the incalculable riches he receives through his membership in the Church, longs to share them with others.

That was one of the principal reasons for our apostolic activity, and with . . . the prospect of moving to the fort, we set about unifying our educational defense in a way comparable to the national reorganization of the armed forces. Not to participate in this corporate enterprise was like going AWOL, and Sister Superior made it clear that privilege, not penalties, should be our incentive.

I had subdued some of my inner restlessness by adapting to the idea of getting the deed for a Golden Jubilee present. Sister Superior thought it was a fine idea, and promised to take it up when she presented her petition for the student chapel.

There really wasn't anything to lose when God was the Chairman of the Board.

CHAPTER XIII

It was only natural that our newly acquired interest in Fort Wright should lead to a study of its history, and here we found much to kindle imagination and strengthen our conviction that God had been looking after us and Holy Names College from the beginning. Long before we had thought of the campaign for a new campus, even before we had moved to our present site and built a College separate from Holy Names Academy and Normal School, a sequence of events was in motion that would ultimately lead to the abandonment of the fort for military purposes and clear the way for us.

As early as 1894, Spokanites had heard that the government was planning to establish another military post in the region and inquired into the possibility of having it in their city. They learned that one thousand acres and water would be necessary, and they fixed upon a popular picnic ground, Twickenham Park, as the best location. The property was available for $40,000, $15,000 of which had to be in cash, and the balance in negotiable land.

With civic zeal the people set about raising the money, but cash was scarce in those days, and the fund grew slowly while War Department officials urged haste. It was the women who finally took a hand and proposed a community Christmas tree, with donated prizes and one-dollar admission tickets, each of which gave the holder a chance on the presents.

This sort of fund-raising seemed so familiar to most of us Sisters that we decided the fort history was taken from our very own book. Even the gift assortment had the same delightfully incongruous ring: a mince pie, a colt, music and painting lessons, curling irons, harmonicas, dental and surgical work, a month's board, rheumatism medicine, paint, pickles, a bicycle, guns and furs.

The whole city backed the project, diligent as nuns, and all the social clubs in the city played cards for tickets. On the last night of the year when most Sisters are making a Holy Hour in the convent chapel while other people celebrate, the townsfolk gathered in the civic auditorium for the prize drawing. The first gift pulled was a pound of tea, followed later by a bull pup and a case of beer. The circulation manager of one city newspaper drew a year's subscription to his own publication, and the local postmaster's loyal purchase of forty tickets netted a woman's hat and two pictures. A maiden lady won a shotgun worth $125 on a ticket that had been given to her, and a man who paid double price to buy a ticket he dreamed was the winning number for a gold watch, had a musical descent into reality when he won a twenty-five-cent harmonica.

We explored the newspaper files with adventurous glee and knew that the spirit of such a history would undoubtedly repeat itself as we built and furnished new classrooms on the proceeds from rummage sales, card parties, widows' mites and stubborn hope.

Cash receipts for this all-out community Christmas tree

amounted to $4,500, and the fort's location was assured, so far as Spokane's part was concerned.

Finally, two years later (at a tempo we had since learned to appreciate) Congress authorized $100,000 for construction, and building began a year after that when the Sisters of the Holy Names had been in Spokane just nine years.

What few persons knew then, and what became public knowledge a quarter-century later, was that the federal government had authorized Fort Wright as a regimental post and that officer quarters, barracks and warehouses for two battalions were literally stolen from beneath the planners' noses and appropriated for Fort Warren, Cheyenne, Wyoming.

Even in 1957, when the whole story came out in *Spokesman-Review* headlines, most readers didn't know how or why this had happened. But we did, even if it was only by hindsight. Colonel George S. Clarke, retired fort commander, was certain that, had the post had full regimental status, it would have been expanded into a brigade post. In that case, it would never have been declared surplus. So it looked as if God was "writing straight with crooked lines" long before most of us had learned how to read.

Legislators from the State of Washington, for some reason, failed to discover what was going on, and it was left to the commanding officer, Colonel McNamara, to learn the hard way. The Roosevelt administration, organizing the Civilian Conservation Corps, sent him an order stating that, three days later, 28,000 men would arrive at Fort Wright for placement in forest camps.

Here, too, the Sisters smiled with recognition, for life in the convent is often as uncertain as in the military, and we had more than once had a smaller army of nuns descend upon us for a convention or a retreat or summer session with little more advance notice than the poor colonel had received. But unlike Colonel McNamara, who suffered a stroke from the shock of such an impossible order, local superiors usually received the news with an act of faith and an appeal to the Sisters to rally round and help out in the emergency.

Somewhere in the attic or storeroom of most convents there's a collection of cots, folding beds, spare mattresses and mismatched springs, for we rarely throw anything useful away, and furnishings replaced by newer, more comfortable pieces are almost certain to be restored to active duty as the religious family grows. A little adroit juggling of bedroom furnishings, a portable partition of some sort, and classrooms and music practice rooms are turned into sleeping apartments by night, while doubling in their usual function by day. In some parochial schools, pastors solicitous for the comfort of hard-working Sisters have calculated the size of the rooms with such precision that nothing except double-deckers could convert a single room to a double one.

Colonel Clarke was left to carry on at Fort George Wright, and he immediately had blueprints prepared and applied for permission to build non-commissioned officer quarters. He was told that Washington, D.C., wouldn't permit tearing down old buildings and replacing them with new ones. When he replied that there were no buildings on the locations designated, he thought the matter would be settled. Instead, it was the beginning of a correspondence as bulky as Sister Superior's later file on the fort. Original blueprints of Fort Wright showed that it had been constructed as a regimental post, the federal officials insisted, and they sent four high-ranking quartermaster officers to investigate. When they couldn't find the buildings, a board of staff officers followed, and the mystery was finally solved.

According to Colonel Clarke's story, Senator Francis E. Warren, father-in-law of General Pershing and chairman of the senate's powerful military affairs committee, had the original bill amended to authorize a regimental post in his home state. In some unknown way, fifty officer quarters, forty non-commissioned officer quarters, six barracks and supplementary operational buildings were also whisked off to Wyoming.

Although the feature writer who interviewed Colonel Clarke and told his story repeatedly professed amazement, it hardly seemed more fantastic to us than the possibility of our own peacetime occupation of the historic site.

The whole situation was so solidly rooted in improbabilities that we wouldn't have been surprised to wake up some morning and find the missing buildings resurrected, filling the gaps of what Colonel Clarke called the "toothless post" with structures as convincing and insubstantial as the ghost towns in a Hollywood western. Still, it seemed more to the point to plan a few buildings of our own instead of indulging a fondness for miracles.

Our architect worked hard building in air, for there was

as yet little solid ground under his sketches. He was an un-communicative and singularly modest man, and he didn't tell us much about his own part in the fort story, information someone had to dig out of newspaper files.

Spokanites had originally wanted the fort in their area to insure protection against hostile Indians. It was named for Colonel George Wright, whose Ninth United States Infantry had camped in the area in 1858 after winning the Battle of Spokane Plains.

In 1935 a portrait of the famous Indian fighter was painted as a federal works project and presented to the fort. The original presentation was made by a person dele-gated to represent the administrator of the federal art program. He was our architect, Henry C. Bertelsen.

And now, instead of giving us pictures of Indians, the architect was bringing pictures of classroom buildings and libraries and dining halls. I remembered all the sketches he had made of chapels that were never built because some new uncertainty, added to the perpetual uncertainty of inadequate funds, had postponed action. First, we had hoped to get permanent vacation of a dead-end street and put a chapel up at the end of Boone Avenue. Next, we had talked of placing it behind the administration building or in front.

One way of restoring a sense of proportion when the out-look was discouraging was to browse through the fort his-tory as if it were the local chronicle kept in every house of our congregation, and search for parallels. It seemed to me that there were many leaves that one might liken to the convent book: two changes of name and several of function. Personnel and commanding officers seemed to come and go by appointments as regular and as incomprehensible as the annual "obedience," which assigns the Sisters of a province to their posts for the coming year. Human nature being what it is, each successive administration introduced changes in the physical plant that were always called improvements, whether they were or not, and appropriate bits of legislation were enacted as need arose. For example: "There will be no shooting of buffalo from second-story windows of barracks."

I wasn't under any illusions regarding the cost. One hundred per cent discount or not, we had already paid a great deal in the waiting and the uncertainty, and I knew we should pay a great deal more in physical labor and financial risk. But "use" and "value" were such slippery terms, their definitions so different, depending on the point of view. For nuns, who still believe in absolutes, nothing undertaken in a genuinely apostolic spirit could be useless. Success and failure, as the world measures them, were relative terms, and the ultimate success lay in the accomplishment of God's Will as fully and as perfectly as possible.

Since the city had originally given the fort land to the federal government and was now unable to get it back without paying for it, I hoped that we could give part of it back through a more intensive program of community service. Perhaps we might do something to preserve the historical character of the site along with the usual contributions a college makes to the people of its area. And I wondered whether we could involve the townspeople in the development of the College.

We wanted to keep whatever historic names already were in use at the fort: Custer Drive, Wright Avenue, Fremont Drive. We hoped to fuse a little of our own community heritage with the history and call some of the halls by the family names of our foundresses.

So the Majors and the Colonels would be painted out, and in their place the visitor might read Durocher, not for the baseball player, but for our own foundress, Mother Marie Rose. You might wander down an avenue named for Wright, the famous Indian fighter, and come to a duplex named Davignon Hall for a nun, a famous Indian teacher. Mother Mary Veronica of the Crucifix had been the first Oregon provincial and a hall would bear her name. Other dormitories were named Ceré and Dufresne, for two other foundresses. It was beginning to sound like the French and Indian wars!

Besides the Colonel Wright monument, there were other "landmarks" at the fort—some of them known to us only through secondhand accounts, as we had been so occupied with the conquest of our own territory that we had not explored beyond it.

Though we hadn't found any pinups, we ran across a pair of marble maidens in the newspaper files, if not in the stone.

A columnist had been trying to uncover the ladies' past and appealed for help from early residents of the city. One reader said that her father, a potter who had made the bricks for the original Fort Wright around 1890, might have made the statues.

She inquired discreetly whether the ladies were clad. "If there are any grape leaves on them," she confided, "I'll wager my dad did them. I found a whole box of his molds in the attic."

But a retired superintendent of shops from the base had the final word. Not only did he know where the girls came from but he knew their names.

"Why, that's Lilian and Sadie Bess!" he said with authority. "No, no, they're nobody special—except I think maybe they're friends of Mercury. They were standing on each side of him out at Baxter Hospital. When Baxter was dismantled they put Mercury in front of the hospital at Fairchild Air Force Base—and we took the girls to George Wright."

The informant said that at one time every new recruit wanted his picture taken next to them to send home. And he himself was the maidens' best friend. Every winter he used to wrap straw and burlap around them.

After reading that story I could see what a shock it must be for old-timers to go out to the fort looking for Lilian and Sadie Bess and come face to face with—St. Joseph.

CHAPTER XIV

Some time in June a strike-it-right publisher sent every one on our faculty a mailer that asked in giant red letters, "MOVING TO A NEW LOCATION?"

It was like having your brain lighted up by a ghoulish kind of fluoroscope to see that unanswerable question leering at you from the bulletin board, from the top of the counter, from the pages of the textbook you picked up hurriedly on the way to summer classes.

So far we had two sets of "interim neighbors" and when life within-doors became too burdensome, I used to sit on our imaginary front porch and look at the Lutherans and the National Guard. I could see them dimly through forests of federalese, office memos, long-distance phone calls, legal phrases and wholly private speculations. The guardsmen were olive drab and motionless, entrenched behind their guns. I suspected they might stay. The Lutherans were less clearly defined. What I heard from them came mostly through Pastor Beck, a kindly pleasant man who called Sister Superior whenever he learned anything more regarding fort disposal and who soon came to receive a similar courtesy from her.

Who might move into the other areas adjoining our property we didn't know, but it was an interesting topic to discuss.

Sister Clotilde thought that a gravel pit would keep us from missing the Great Northern Railway. With a little effort, she maintained, a cement mixer and whatever else they used in gravel pits could do just as good a job interrupting lectures as a line of boxcars. If the noise disturbed too much, the class could always go out for a field trip.

The railroad, which had so often interrupted class lectures at Holy Names College, continued to exercise its delaying action with respect to the new College campus. The company owned a spur extending into the section of property we wanted, and we had to wait for the owners to have a survey. The first one disclosed that the tracks were out of bounds, and more time passed in coordinating the two surveys and reassigning boundaries. Only then was a complete legal description possible.

The National Guard area had previously necessitated a readjustment of our boundaries, and I began to feel that we would be multimillionaires if, like the poet, we could be "monarch of all [we] survey."

Psychology and sociology teachers pondered the prospect of facilities for the mentally ill and for alcoholics on remaining fort property. The Director of Admissions brightened visibly whenever residential development was mentioned. That idea appealed to the treasurer, too, because she was sure that incorporation into the City of Spokane would follow, and we'd have no more worries about utilities and city services.

One of Gonzaga's top graduates, a candidate for a doctorate at Georgetown, applied for a position in our philosophy department. To a thorough knowledge of Latin and Greek, he added the accomplishments of a musician. We explained that he might have to join the peripatetic school and offered him a contract.

We had taken a deep breath and announced the Fort Wright Summer Theatre where high school juniors and seniors might live the theatre and earn advanced credit toward college. By concentrating on an area that normally had to take second place to their regular high school studies, they could progress more rapidly and learn something about all phases of the art: acting, costume design, set construction, play production. The experience might help young people in their choice of a college major. The program was to be coeducational, and besides introducing prospective students to Holy Names College, it might also develop an acting pool from which male players could be recruited for later College productions. Even after the flyers were out the deed had not arrived, and we began thinking of ways to explain why the Fort Wright Summer Theatre might not be at Fort Wright.

The sergeant looked in to say that road-clearing equipment was available at low cost if we'd act now, and though it didn't seem very useful in early June, we could still remember the January snows. It woudn't be the same at the fort as in town where an accommodating city commissioner had sent the snowplows out at eleven o'clock one winter night so that the Sisters attending a meeting at our College wouldn't need skis to get over the snow-mountains piled along the curbing.

Two Sisters began spending their Saturdays at the fort setting out plants and flowers so that we'd be able to decorate the altar in a chapel still in the Mind of God.

If possible we hoped for something more satisfactory than the "garden" described by an Irish postulant who made her novitiate in New York. Unaccustomed to the crowded city life she looked forward eagerly to a sojourn in Long Island, where, the Sisters said enthusiastically, the convent had a lovely yard and a garden.

When the postulant entered this earthly paradise, her memories of the rolling hills of Ireland still fresh and green, she asked to see the garden. They led her to a standard square yard (thirty-six inches) where ten Sisters walked around a single rose bush under the shadow of the Manhattan skyline.

Sister Superior asked the bishop to give us a resident chaplain, preferably with chapel, as we'd no longer be able to expect Gonzaga to send a Jesuit. We had missed our chance to bid on the base chapel, a frame building large enough for 250. With other temporary structures, it had been up for auction at a time when we still had no ground, even temporary, to put under it. Moving it would be more expensive than buying it, and it was out of the question to keep it "on ice" on Boone Avenue until we did or didn't have some fort land. The federal government was in a hurry to clear off the wooden structures, and we had no permission to buy extras.

So we had said good-bye to our hopes for a larger chapel and tried to believe that we would get something better before a century elapsed. When the provincial bursar visited the fort site, inspected the chapel, and conferred with the contractor, we were instructed to bid on the building. But by that time, we had already lost out to the pastor of the Salvation Inn for All Nations, who had produced the required cash down payment.

The Reverend Mr. Turner had raised enough money to buy the chapel but not enough to move it. He asked for and received an extension of time to gather funds for the project. Months passed, and though he collected more, he still lacked the necessary sum and risked losing the payment he had already made.

Sister Superior called him and asked whether he wanted the building taken off his hands. He was unwilling to give up, so she extended her sympathy and the promise of prayers. There was no insincerity or duplicity in her attitude. She did indeed believe unfalteringly that whatever is, is adorable, that the Will of God works its mysterious ends in seemingly arbitrary and accidental events. Her attention focused not so much on her own desire to get the chapel as on the plight of the disappointed pastor.

We had already had some friendly interference from the fire department the preceding year when inspectors pronounced third-floor bedrooms unsafe without fire escapes. Since we would need to use all available duplexes for dormitories if we moved everything out to the fort, we decided that we had better know the worst. We invited the fire chief to go over the buildings and decide what we would have to do to bring them up to standard. As a matter of course we expected him to tell us to add fire escapes. His answer was electrifying: we needed fire escapes plus a complete rewiring job!

We reread the clause about not being able to claim compensation for improvements made on the property in the event that the interim agreement were terminated. We looked again at the calendar; at our boxes and boxes of scientific apparatus and library books and audio-visual aids and art materials and darkroom equipment; at the furniture, utensils and school supplies still in active use; and at the mountains of miscellany yet to be tracked down and boxed and labeled for delivery to a land we did not own, where there might be a chaplain if we somehow found a chapel, in a College that didn't even have a definite name.

I had wanted to announce the name change at our commencement in June. It seemed to me that the final graduation from our present campus (if indeed it were the last) had a value as history, and that it was newsworthy. I reasoned that to announce the change of name then might rate a little more notice than at some other time, and we would have a start toward establishing the change in the mind of the public. But at the last minute, superiors decided that such an announcement would be premature.

It was clearly too late to build a library in time for fall classes, and we didn't know where, on the eighty-five acres we'd asked for, anything even temporarily suitable could be found. It seemed ironic in view of the fact that the librarian had been among the first to do serious paper work on her space needs. She had secured floor plans for every likely building on our various "claims" and had de-vised a system for fitting scale models of shelves and tables into the rooms. Through this method and consultation with other librarians, she had successively chosen and re-jected the jail, the base exchange and one or two other possibilities.

"Where's the library this week?" came to be a standard query whenever the librarian joined her Sisters, and every building she approached called for that same appraising look. In her lexicon, more lastingly than all Gaul divided into three parts, stood all space divided among 20,000 vol-umes. Unless there was room to grow after that, she headed inexorably for larger quarters.

Summer heat blazed down on the Inland Empire, and for a few weeks the treasurer stopped having nightmares about thirty-five furnaces. The trials of falling thermom-eters and frozen pipes seemed more remote.

But still the deed did not come.

We had been praying thirty-eight months for a piece of paper that would be the end of all our troubles—or the beginning of them—and the cold war went on and end-lessly on with empty diplomatic phrases riding the mails from Washington, D.C., to Washington State, and the cold cry of naked faith rising uninterruptedly to a hidden God.

Mindful of the exchange between President Kennedy and Cardinal Spellman regarding federal aid to private schools, some Sisters had hoped that the deed would arrive before Kennedy had been long in office. There was no tell-ing what hasty withdrawal of present favors might result if the opposition made enough noise for him to pay attention. One or two intrepid Stay-Put-ers still talked of the possibility of Providential interference with a plan that might not be altogether prudent. While they continued to dispense cold water I thought of Seward's Folly and felt more businesslike than usual.

We teased the linen keeper about her presidential protégé and told her we felt sure that he must be to blame for the delay. And after that we noticed that she stayed even longer in chapel than formerly, as if she felt personally responsible for whatever part Kennedy might have in holding up Holy Names College development. She made sacrifices too—ingenious ones like giving up her verbal blasts against modern art—and she offered them for the document that was always out of sight but seldom out of mind.

Somebody discovered at War Surplus some material similar to monk's cloth, available for a few cents a yard, and Sister Superior began counting windows and authorized purchase of one thousand yards, while Sister Phillip took a new interest in drapery designs and silk screen printing, and Sister Edward calculated the labor required to launder and stitch. The fabric had been twisted on the bolt and stretched on the bias, but Sister Edward, nothing daunted, posted signs in the girls' dormitory advertising "curtain bees" and the students drifted down to the school art lab to help the Sisters pull the material back into shape, remove some unwanted stitching, and cut the cloth into lengths manageable for washing and ironing.

Summer session had begun by the time the curtains were ready to launder, and the Sisters from other schools summoned their community spirit and devoted hours to sewing and ironing in preparation for an uncertain future. As it became obvious that even a massive effort would be inadequate to complete the task with our limited laundry facilities, an enterprising Sister discovered a local laundromat where do-it-yourself found more effective mechanical assistance. Soon afterward, a black procession wound its daily way to the establishment, and the Sisters quickly became experienced enough to feel that they could set up as drapery specialists.

Meanwhile, Sister Phillip directed the paint-making and stenciling process that came next, and then all the draperies had to be ironed again in order to fix the color. The work proceeded at intervals through the day, in crowded workrooms, and for hours each night in the hot summer weather.

Sometimes, looking at Sister Phillip's paint-stained sleeves and the dark circles around her eyes, I wondered whether it was worth it. But I had to admit that some kind of window covering was indispensable, and newspapers probably would not do. If I decided that we should buy all the draperies ready-made, I had only to look at department store prices and do some simple arithmetic to learn how impossible that seemed.

Kitchen curtains would help to make the place livable, and the Sister in charge of home economics was commissioned to do something about that. It would be an assembly-line job, just a matter of making curtains for about twenty windows in ten kitchens of five identical duplexes. With her customary caution she went to do some checking before cutting the material and discovered that, though all the windows were identical from the outside, cupboards and built-ins had modified them on the inside. She ended up with custom-made curtains for each kitchen. If we didn't move to the fort, maybe we could construct a building with windows made to fit the curtains.

We had worn a permanent rut in all the approaches to the fort property, and when we took our college cars out of the garage, like horses heading home for pasture, they pointed northwest without any human intervention. The usual way led out Boone Avenue, to a right turn on Nettleton, beyond Colonel Clarke's home and over the bridge to the fort. The frame buildings were thinning out now, and Officers' Row looked considerably less bleak than when we had moved in our family of forty-seven pioneers.

Once in a while, with the sun falling at the proper angle, with squirrels frisking about in the aging evergreens and magpies lifting their raucous cries against invasion, it seemed like a chapter out of Josue as we camped on the uncertain borders of our Promised Land.

I went out one day with Sister Maria, and we parked The Jewel for a few lingering minutes and looked at the fort land laid out below us and remembered our first disheartening introduction. There was no doubt about it: we had actually fallen in love with the place, and we hoped soon to be sending out to our Sisters everywhere a photographic record of our future home with running commentary.

❉   ❉   ❉   ❉

Sister Edward had insisted that no one who saw Fort Wright clothed in the glory of a Spokane snowfall could hold out longer than five minutes against the move.

"Let's go out to the fort and take some pictures," she had said to me one Sunday morning, when our first heavy snow of the season clung, fragile and untouched, to the evergreens; and the sun, just coming through, worked its witchery of sparkle and shadow. Thirty minutes later, it would start to melt, and now was the time to capture those breathtaking angularities and delicate drifts.

Getting ready for the weather and the pictures was like slipping into harness: unbelievably complicated the first time, but easy enough with practice. I slung the brown Rollei strap over my black veil. I pulled the veil free in back so I could turn my head without feeling that I was on a bridle, and secured the camera with my right hand to keep it from banging into things. Then I fumbled into galoshes and a wadded winter cape, stuffed my pockets with film and flashbulbs, and hung the lens mount of the flashgun from one gloved finger.

Thus accoutered, I was not the most graceful creature in sight, but I was ready to shoot snow scenes. Meanwhile, Sister Edward had collected the Ford keys, Sister Phillip, a 35-millimeter camera, some color film, and an Office book, for she had not gone beyond Matins, and there might be a few minutes to park and pray beneath the arching branches where God seemed very near. So many of the Psalms and Canticles in the Little Office of the Blessed Virgin rang with renewed significance amid the natural beauties to which they often allude. Surrounded by the glories of His creation, we could heed the Psalmist's invitation to *"glorify the Lord with exultation . . . lift up our voice to the Rock of our salvation . . . enter into His presence with praises, with songs . . . glorify Him/ For the*

Lord is the great God and the great King above all gods: in His hand are the depths of the earth, and the heights of the mountains are His./ His is the sea: for He made it, and the dry land, which His hands have formed."

We loaded our film on the way to the fort and watched for camera angles as we neared the main gate where the road curved around a familiar cluster of buildings. Deciduous trees still kept the intricate tracery of twigs that precedes and follows winter, and a soft-focus version of silver thaw ransomed the meanest weed from acres of oblivion.

We pulled off the road between steep embankments, unable to pass the sheer fall of white, the dark ribbon of road, the lift of dense green fir, crested with incredible softness. Sister Edward backed the car out of camera range, and I struggled up the incline to crouch uncertainly in a snowdrift and see what was in my lens. Far down the road, Sister Phillip made a black blob against the hillside, as she looked for a likely color shot. An air force car swung round the bend, coming toward us, and the men seemed about to volunteer to tow Sister Edward to a service station when they sighted me sliding down the hill, very careful to protect the camera. They smiled, waved, and left us to our photographic devices.

We clicked our way past a rediscovered river, down avenues of enchantment, toward buildings branched about by miracle, and we gave it all back to the Giver in the Canticle of the Three Children: "O dews and hoar frosts, bless the Lord: O frost and cold, bless the Lord./ O ice and snow, bless the Lord . . . let us praise and exalt Him above all forever."

We saw His majesty in the sweep of hill and sky; His

splendor in the dazzle of sun on snow; His delicacy in the filigree of flake on hollow and thorn. We marvelled at His goodness in giving us so much that was beautiful, and our hearts were uplifted with Christian hope, as we prayed over this transfigured world: *"Lord, it is good for us to be here: if Thou wilt, let us make here three tabernacles. . . ."* More than ever, we wanted this property, but we wanted it in order to make it more truly His, to hold in trust, as it were, for all the young women who might learn, in this exquisite setting, that sacramental view of the universe which seemed so inescapable to us at the present moment.

We sloshed home cold and wet, hopeful and happy, convinced that we could withstand any opposition from within our ranks, for the transformations wrought in the winter world of the fort were not to be compared with the liabilities of a few loosened shingles or sagging porches.

* * * *

Now we were still waiting. We knew that the waiting could not last forever, but it seemed like a reasonable facsimile of forever. I thought about Thomas Merton's sentences on hope—the perfect hope that we achieve on the brink of despair "when, instead of falling over the edge, we find ourselves walking on the air." We walked on it then. We built campus castles in it. We filled our lungs with it, and life was good.

Across the river, the Land of Promise stretched out, golden in the simple light of June. Faint and faraway it seemed, this impossible goal of a Chosen People, alternately led and pursued by an exacting Love. In the intensive glow of that fleeting vision, doubt vanished and infinite hope was born.

Unreality? Perhaps . . . or possibly a kind of super-reality, something you can test by asking if it works, as this instant of recognition subsequently did.

Situated on a rise, the land followed the curve of the Spokane River, where the narrow stream wound, placid and energetic by turns, toward city center to tumble with frontier informality over Spokane Falls. Looking due east, the city itself spread out before the eye: the red brick crenelations of the ancient *Spokesman-Review* building; the sheer glass-punctuated facade of a newer department store; the height of scattered apartment buildings in a community where housing was still more than adequate for the population.

Beyond the river, looking northwest, the campanile of St. Charles Church pointed skyward. Nearby, the church itself spread fantastic wings for a flight into the super-natural. The air was brisk and bright with challenge, and avenues of trees followed the road where it looped about the parade ground to focus on a slim white shaft that looked deserted without the Stars and Stripes.

The parallels between our journey into the unknown and that of the Israelites appeared to me to be multiplying every day. Perhaps I was living in a fantasy-world, though I do not think so. God speaks to His people today through sign and symbol in a different but nonetheless real manner. He makes use of our human intelligence and our natural powers to work out His designs. Seldom does He deal with us in the direct and wholly miraculous manner in which He appeared to Moses and the prophets, for we have the revelation of His Divine Son to guide us. But He is never far from those who wait upon His Wisdom, never heedless of those who call upon Him in trust.

But for those who viewed matters in the cold dry light of practicality the College still looked about as substantial as a mirage. Reporters checked frequently on building plans, knowing that we couldn't possibly carry on our classes without some modifications. They thought we were holding out when we were merely holding on. Our architect seemed a little restless under this prolonged session of window-shopping, and even the salesmen knocked opportunities to peddle their wares in a world of shifting sands.

Whenever I felt disposed to think that we would be better off if we had never heard of Fort Wright, I'd find myself considering a slight figure, inclined intently toward the tabernacle, as Sister Superior drew on the resources she understood best and that were, after all, those on which our lives as Christians, and still more as nuns, ought to be built.

I looked around for every bit of "color" that could plug the holes where solid news stories ought to go, and in the absence of information and a future, I substituted parallels and the past.

On the parade ground, safely within our hoped-for property line, was a huge megaphone mounted on a pivot, through which in years gone by a bugler had sounded all his signals from reveille to taps. Judging by the noises I had heard coming from the wind instruments class the previous summer, I felt sure that a Sister could be found somewhere to summon the community to prayer by something other than a bell. It might come in handy for intermissions between classes too, until we installed an intercom and bell system.

A student overheard the neighborhood druggist, who hoped we wouldn't move and take away all that lovely trade, and we promptly asked him to double his advertisement in our College newspaper. As publications adviser, I wondered how we'd reach our advertising quota without the neighborhood stores to buy space. We'd had personal delivery service from our printer, too, since he had to pass by the College each day on his way to and from work.

We dragged dishes and furniture out to the base exchange for the seventh "last time" to entertain some other group that wanted to see the fort and was certain to do us immeasurable good in consequence. The building had been refurbished at bargain basement rates under the shrewd direction of the Sister in charge of fort development. She had borrowed panels of knotty pine from an unwanted partition to cover the scars left by a severed counter. Then she had masked another riddled section with a gigantic oil painting in a massive frame. The picture had been too large for any room in the College building to support, but at the first public gathering at the fort, it hung happily opposite the chair of the donor, the secretary for the women's auxiliary.

The Sisters spent many days cleaning and recleaning "Greystones," the newly-named base exchange, scrubbing floors underneath the carpenters, to the accompaniment of drifting sawdust and the measured spray of two or three quarts of indispensable paint.

Made alphabet conscious by her contacts with service personnel, the Sister builder of Holy Names College had taken one sharp look at the tall blue letters over the entrance reading BASE EXCHANGE. Shortly after they read BASE EX   A GE and finally HNC.

She served brunch or dinner as if she were a veteran employee of a restaurant that specialized in Chicken to Go, and everything was done with such aplomb that patrons naturally supposed we had full-scale kitchen and refrigeration facilities.

The alumnae, often the last converts to a break in tradition, brought their husbands and children out to the fort for "Kiddie Day." They enjoyed refreshments in Greystones, tag on the parade ground, baseball on the diamond and a steady parental workout pushing swings. They had gone home happily enthusiastic, promising to join us in praying for the legal title, when a man drove up in a truck to what he thought was the abandoned site. Coolly he proceeded to the playground carrying some obviously efficient tools, evidently with the intention of removing the swings and other play equipment.

Before he could sever a link, the Sister sentry had riveted her attention on the truck and the tools.

"May I ask what you're doing?" she asked in a way that plainly said, "I may."

"I'm just going to remove this playground equipment," he answered, teetering toward a seesaw and gripping a large hammer.

"Oh, no," said the sentry. "I'm afraid you can't do that. You'll have to bring written authorization before you can take anything from this property." She looked toward the non-commissioned officers' quarters hoping for sight of the sergeant.

"If you go right over there," she said pointing, "you'll find the officer in charge. Maybe he can have several Air Force boys help you." She smiled encouragingly; he turned round with his tools and went back to the truck on his way to anywhere else. Happily, we never saw him again.

Mother Provincial sent our assignments for the following year and, with them, a few surprises. Sister Superior would stay on as president, but she would relinquish her duties as Superior to someone else. Another Superior would preside over a small community in the present College administration building, and the College faculty would presumably "pick up their tents like the Arabs" and drift away silently toward Fort Wright.

I amused myself with an interior design for Holy Names College for Nomads with classrooms that went together by musical magic like the reconstructed Teahouse of the August Moon. I worked out another plan for staggering 160 classes over a twenty-four-hour day of a seven-day week so that one, two or three classrooms would be enough, and no class would meet for less than two sessions a week. I moved quonsets in my dreams, hard-hearted millionaires in my imagination, and mountains in my prayers. Some of the mountains started to look like superiors, so I quit. I told Sister Superior what she already knew, and still the deed did not come.

The flagpole was empty—tantalizingly so—rising like an elongated monument over the relics of our crumbling hope.

CHAPTER XV

We live in an age when the forces that divide men are trying to crowd out those that make them one. In a sense this has been true of human history ever since the Fall of Adam. But as the barriers of language, culture and physical distance lower, the cleavage in ideas and ideals becomes even more apparent. That is why mutual understanding has always seemed to me so important and why I have been waging my own particular Cold War against the notion that nuns are not really people.

What Thomas Merton told Mark Van Doren about Trappists is true of nuns, too: our job here is to be more ourselves, not less. The more truly we are ourselves, the less dependent we shall be on the opinion of others, on status and conformity. We shall be more free in the best sense of the word, and with this freedom will come the release of energies we hardly suspected we had.

Eugene Burdick, co-author of *The Ugly American*, has said that Americans stand at a crossroads where they must recover their capacity to take risks, to meet challenges, not with corps of specialists, but with the individual resourcefulness and tough-minded practicality of our forebears. And this is what American Sisters are still trying to do, as anyone who knows them well can testify.

The protests against allocating fort property to the Lutherans and to us had died down. There had been a few reader letters published on both sides, but we preferred to make no answer other than our continuing effort to ransom the land and the buildings from neglect and vandalism. We were on the side of all those townspeople and service men who wanted to restore the fort to its prime.

A group of inspectors from General Services Administration came to look over our "settlement" and were visibly impressed with the transformation we had effected with minimum expenditures in so short a time. They drove round "The Key" past a solidly enshrined St. Joseph, noted the well-kept lawn, the spray forming a rainbow curtain behind the statue, and the flowers blooming at its feet. They listened sympathetically to our construction problems and assured us that the deed would be forthcoming. Only technicalities were responsible for the delay. We urged our need to go ahead with renovation and new building, our reluctance to begin until the title was clear. They promised to do what they could.

Pastor Beck, meanwhile, had declared his intention of erecting a new Lutheran school, having found Building 602 unsatisfactory in view of remodeling estimates. Sister Superior told him of our need, and he agreed to take up with the board the possibility of lending us space for a year. Such a solution would be a major help: we needed classrooms desperately. We also needed a library and a chapel.

We decided that to put a Catholic chapel in one wing of the Lutheran building might be pushing inter-faith cooperation a little too hard. That left a choice between library and classrooms.

A new version of crossing the bar was enacted when we lent Greystones to Pastor Beck for a Lutheran youth rally, and the boys brought sleeping bags into the former tap-room before the huge stone fireplace to spend the night. We took lessons in a more effective type of church support when the Lutherans opened their building for public inspection the Sunday after receiving the interim permit. They wanted church members to see the work that needed to be done, whereas we had been unwilling to put the buildings on display until they were scrubbed and furnished.

The Sister whom obedience had assigned as new Superior, the inheritor of vast uncertainties, decided to visit Spokane and learn at first hand the proportions of her task. She cast an experienced and objective eye over the work she saw there. Then she returned quietly to Marylhurst to present a detached appraisal: the transfer of the College in the three months that remained was not difficult. It was impossible.

Two weeks later she returned, having been relieved of her teaching assignment at the Marylhurst College summer session, to get a month's head start on the impossible. She took up her residence in Spokane for Operation Exodus, the greatest all-out effort of the Holy Names Sisters since the first beachhead on the Oregon Coast in 1859. Working with the Sister president, she mapped out strategy for the move. She also enlisted volunteers for post-summer session and Saturday chores.

Not too long after, the sound of hammers rang out like an anvil chorus from the warehouses; bulldozers and "pushcats" crawled over mounds of earth, and workmen were preparing to pour foundations for a small classroom and assembly building. What began that day ended in a bill for $400,000. The deed was still not in our hands. But it didn't matter any more because everything was irretrievably in the Hands of God.

The bishop agreed to give us a chaplain whom we referred to tentatively as a "pastor of souls" since we were sure we had souls.

Pastor Beck called to say that the board had agreed to our using space in 602, rent free, and he also arranged for us to use kitchen and refrigeration facilities until ours were ready. It meant that we had to take food by foot or by jeep to the cafeteria in Greystones, but we were already in training for that, and it was much easier than bringing it from the kitchens in town.

With characteristic energy Sister Clotilde had engineered a clean-up and moving party for education majors before classes dismissed in June. We tried to tell her that it would be an anticlimax if they had to bring everything back again before fall. But she was adamant. She wouldn't be around in the fall, and it was now or never. God would simply have to be reasonable about things.

Somewhere in the middle of all that muddle, in the fiftieth month after we had first started to dream of moving to Fort George Wright, in a morning mail left lying for a couple of hours on the president's desk and looking no different from any other, the deed came. Sister Superior held it in her hand for a minute. She looked thoughtfully toward the corner where her secretary sat tapping out her

Friday morning responses at the typewriter. Outside, a lawnmower whirred pleasantly, and the smell of cut grass drifted through the open window. The next day would be the twenty-sixth anniversary of her religious vows. She took the envelope with her and slipped quietly into the chapel. Then she asked the secretary to ring the bell and summon the community for a *Te Deum* of thanksgiving.

Once the moving started, it seemed there would be no end: neighbors moved to kindliness and charity; skeptics moved to conviction; rivals moved to unselfishness; contemplatives moved to action; a Provident God moved to compassion; and the Brides of Christ moved to a deeply apostolic and burning love.

Our Sisters flocked from all over the city to help. Boys from the preparatory seminary lent a hand. Jesuit scholastics joined the troops. Boys from the parish grade school ran errands and carried grade school loads. Alumnae turned out with husbands or helpful children—or, in one case, with five gentleman friends and trucks to increase their effectiveness.

Administrators of the College decided to reward the Sister recruits with a party, one of those simple gatherings where nuns can have fun without elaborate preparations. The new superior presented workers with "stock" in Fort Wright in recognition of their services.

More substantial than the counterfeit stock was the pledge from higher superiors that the provincialate would assume the debt on the administration building. Its name would be changed to Convent of the Holy Names, and twenty-four Sisters would live there while the Academy used classrooms to relieve its space shortage. Holy Names Academy, in turn, would make a cash payment and assume the unpaid debt on Marian Hall, where it would house high school boarders.

As for the College, with such a brief history as an independent institution, the question of continuity seemed important. Its name, therefore, would be Holy Names College at Fort Wright, a designation we hoped might establish in the public mind the transfer to a new campus.

The librarian found three Sisters to help her paint reading room walls in the Lutheran building, thus paving the way for future identification as "the Sister who works for the Lutherans." Truckloads of books continued to arrive from the East Campus, and nobody worried about whether we'd have to do the whole job over again when we got around to building our own library the following year.

The incoming Sister Superior and the outgoing Sister Superior made an active team. Engaged in a different kind of desk work, they dropped a desk on the retiring superior's toe, and she was promoted briefly to a white-collar job where she could read *Leisure, The Basis of Culture* and ponder, without a trace of self-pity, the need for time to reflect.

I thought of the editor of one of the nation's oldest and most distinguished poetry magazines. He had inquired about the retired poet-president of one of the top Catholic colleges for women. Viewing the duties of her administration in retrospect, he sighed.

"She had to worry about all kinds of things," he said mournfully. "Like whether the sprinklers were running on the lawn."

I thought of a less famous but no less wonderful poet-president of a virtually unknown college and wanted to tell him that his friend had advanced a step beyond our president. Ours would not have to remember to tell somebody to turn on the sprinklers: she'd go out herself and turn them on.

But now with reinforcements on the administrative staff, she might look forward to a period of more effective academic leadership. That is, if the transition from East to West Campus could be completed in time for life to settle into a reasonably normal routine.

The Air Force wanted to retain road rights through the fort property to and from Fairchild Air Force Base. We were happy to sanction the arrangement because it meant our roads would be kept cleared even during heavy snowfall.

Fire Chief Durham came out to help in the formal flag raising since not even our star window-cleaning Sister aspired that high. The red engine flashed up in the morning sun to park on the green close to the foot of the pole. Crew members hoisted a man on a three-sectioned 150-foot ladder. He was attached by a safety belt to one section, mounted confidently to its top rung, then shot higher as the second and finally the third section were raised from the truck. Onlookers relived their childhood awe over circus acrobatics, and held their breath during the few minutes required for the fireman to adjust the rope. The sergeant stood by with his friend and co-worker to see that the flag was properly folded. Sisters and College students watched with tightening throats as Old Glory went up and up, to open out beautifully against a brilliant Spokane sky.

The group pledged allegiance and sang "The Star Span-
gled Banner" while killdeer called over the open fields and
geese sailed through the blue air on their way to the river's
edge. As the clear voices lifted over the land of the free, a
breeze rippled the flag and Sister Maria thought she understood why they had come to this home of the brave.

Sister President walked back along the brick walk toward the administration building and watched the students scattering for their classes. She glanced at the wide
verandas running round the six-apartment building that
would be the Sisters' convent. This was the least attractive
of the buildings now in use, but it might easily have been
mistaken for the most attractive by those who observed
how she was drawn to it. For inside the Sisters' convent
was a small oratory where the sanctuary lamp, perpetually
alight, reminded of a Presence no less Real for lack of outward splendor.

The students had attended the Mass of the Holy Spirit
in the assembly building, where the sacristan had set up
the portable altar and prepared everything the celebrant
would need. But there was no question of reserving the
Blessed Sacrament there. The building was in use all day
for classes and programs, for music practice and any gathering larger than thirty students.

When Sister President returned to her office a telephone
message was waiting. She picked up the telephone, dialed
the number, and began to look over the memoranda on her
desk pad.

There was still a long way to go, but the campus was
shaping up. The post bakery had made an attractive Foods

and Nutrition Center. The guest house had been converted to a music building; administration and commissary buildings housed biological sciences and art. A connecting unit between two buildings created additional classroom space, and smaller classes were held in some of the officers' homes not used for dormitories. A dining hall would be among the first urgent needs, as would a library, and. . . .

Salvation waited at the other end of the line. Distractedly, she asked, "Who is it, please?" And then she knew. It was her friend, the pastor of the Salvation Inn for All Nations, and he was announcing glad tidings to his Roman Catholic friend and intercessor.

"Yes, yes, we're still interested. That's too bad." She had to work hard to keep from sounding jubilant. But his admission of defeat was somebody else's victory.

They moved the chapel very soon afterward. It took a week or so to prepare a foundation and ready the white frame building for its journey into our midst. A few trees had to be sacrificed. Power was cut off temporarily, as men moved the building carefully across the road and settled it into place. Looking like a small country church, the chapel that had been a place of worship for Protestant, Catholic and Jewish servicemen rested on its new foundation and was christened Chapel of the Holy Name of Jesus.

EPILOGUE

Six or eight weeks ago, in the deepest depths of winter, one of the Sisters went for a walk to Notre Dame. She brought me home a small twig of ice-buds. A ray of light had glinted off the frozen drops about the nodules, and she wanted me to see and share.

She carried the shoot carefully up to my room where we admired it and placed it on the outside window sill to last as long as ice resisted thaw. Then I brought it in and put it in a medicine bottle on our window sill, less for any faith I had in what it would become than for what it said to me of search and human happiness.

Today five buds, opening like wounds, make a small brightness in the dark of this upper room. They are like those tiny blue flowers you see sometimes pushing up through chinks in sidewalks or jutting out unbelievably from the curbstone. Outside, my "view" is framed by the dull facades of two buildings, with a lower level of tarred roof broken by irregular puddles where its surface dips and rises. Air vents thrust upward here and there, and against the grey sky a smokestack puffs. There is no hint of leaf from here—only the television aerial making a strangely twentieth-century cross.

But inside the dead year seems closer to redemption. For faith and hope and love and beauty are where you find them. They flower quite unexpectedly on the edge of terrifying canyons or mesh their roots with broken bones and human waste. They do not even give up in the inhospitable brick and metal of our cities or in the rubble of our burned-out lives.

We cannot kill the hunger and the emptiness by which man knows his need. But we can keep alive the image of the Creator that is in each of us and so point the way to the true meaning of man.

This is the real task of education at whatever level. This is the reason for the Sister teacher. This is the goal it would be traitorous to relinquish. This is the story of a small Catholic college for women, kept alive by a group of Sisters, kept alive by the love of God.